A PICNIC ON ICE

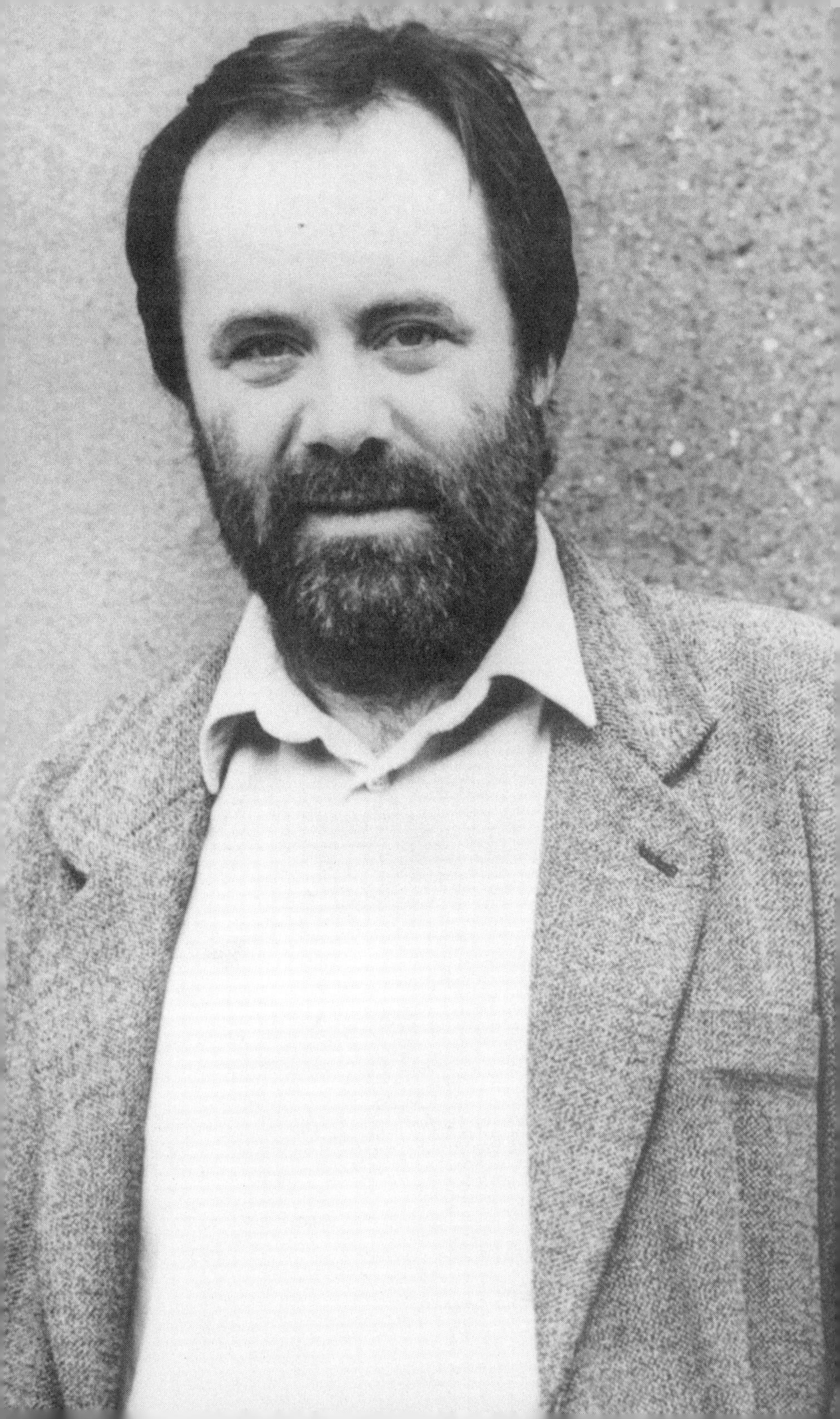

Signal EDITIONS

Carmine Starnino, Editor
Michael Harris, Founding Editor

SELECTED POEMS David Solway
THE MULBERRY MEN David Solway
A SLOW LIGHT Ross Leckie
NIGHT LETTERS Bill Furey
COMPLICITY Susan Glickman
A NUN'S DIARY Ann Diamond
CAVALIER IN A ROUNDHEAD SCHOOL Errol MacDonald
VEILED COUNTRIES/LIVES Marie-Claire Blais (Translated by Michael Harris)
BLIND PAINTING Robert Melançon (Translated by Philip Stratford)
SMALL HORSES & INTIMATE BEASTS Michel Garneau
   (Translated by Robert McGee)
IN TRANSIT Michael Harris
THE FABULOUS DISGUISE OF OURSELVES Jan Conn
ASHBOURN John Reibetanz
THE POWER TO MOVE Susan Glickman
MAGELLAN'S CLOUDS Robert Allen
MODERN MARRIAGE David Solway
K. IN LOVE Don Coles
THE INVISIBLE MOON Carla Hartsfield
ALONG THE ROAD FROM EDEN George Ellenbogen
DUNINO Stephen Scobie
KINETIC MUSTACHE Arthur Clark
RUE SAINTE FAMILLE Charlotte Hussey
HENRY MOORE'S SHEEP Susan Glickman
SOUTH OF THE TUDO BEM CAFÉ Jan Conn
THE INVENTION OF HONEY Ricardo Sternberg
EVENINGS AT LOOSE ENDS Gérald Godin (Translated by Judith Cowan)
THE PROVING GROUNDS Rhea Tregebov
LITTLE BIRD Don Coles
HOMETOWN Laura Lush
FORTRESS OF CHAIRS Elisabeth Harvor
NEW & SELECTED POEMS Michael Harris
BEDROCK David Solway
TERRORIST LETTERS Ann Diamond

THE SIGNAL ANTHOLOGY Edited by Michael Harris
MURMUR OF THE STARS: SELECTED SHORTER POEMS Peter Dale Scott
WHAT DANTE DID WITH LOSS Jan Conn
MORNING WATCH John Reibetanz
JOY IS NOT MY PROFESSION Muhammad al-Maghut
  (Translated by John Asfour and Alison Burch)
WRESTLING WITH ANGELS: SELECTED POEMS Doug Beardsley
HIDE & SEEK Susan Glickman
MAPPING THE CHAOS Rhea Tregebov
FIRE NEVER SLEEPS Carla Hartsfield
THE RHINO GATE POEMS George Ellenbogen
SHADOW CABINET Richard Sanger
MAP OF DREAMS Ricardo Sternberg
THE NEW WORLD Carmine Starnino
THE LONG COLD GREEN EVENINGS OF SPRING Elisabeth Harvor
FAULT LINE Laura Lush
WHITE STONE: THE ALICE POEMS Stephanie Bolster
KEEP IT ALL Yves Boisvert (Translated by Judith Cowan)
THE GREEN ALEMBIC Louise Fabiani
THE ISLAND IN WINTER Terence Young
A TINKERS' PICNIC Peter Richardson
SARACEN ISLAND: THE POEMS OF ANDREAS KARAVIS David Solway
BEAUTIES ON MAD RIVER: SELECTED AND NEW POEMS Jan Conn
WIND AND ROOT Brent MacLaine
HISTORIES Andrew Steinmetz
ARABY Eric Ormsby
WORDS THAT WALK IN THE NIGHT Pierre Morency
  (Translated by Lissa Cowan and René Brisebois)
A PICNIC ON ICE: SELECTED POEMS Matthew Sweeney
HELIX: NEW AND SELECTED POEMS John Steffler
HERESIES: THE COMPLETE POEMS OF ANNE WILKINSON, 1924-1961
  Edited by Dean Irvine

Véhicule Press

www.vehiculepress.com

A Picnic on Ice

SELECTED POEMS

Matthew Sweeney

Signal
EDITIONS

SIGNAL EDITIONS IS AN IMPRINT OF VÉHICULE PRESS

Signal Editions editor: Carmine Starnino
Special assistance: Michael Harris
Cover design: David Drummond
Photograph of the author: Caroline Forbes
Typeset in Minion by Simon Garamond
Printed by AGMV-Marquis Inc.

Copyright © Matthew Sweeney 2002

First published in Great Britain in 2002 by
Jonathan Cape, Random House

CANADIAN CATALOGUING IN PUBLICATION DATA

Sweeney, Matthew, 1952-
   A picnic on ice : selected poems
ISBN: 1-55065-163-3
   1. Title.
PR6069.W37P43 2002   821'.914   C2002-900842-S

Published by Véhicule Press, Montréal, Québec, Canada
www.vehiculepress.com

Distributed by General Distribution Services

Printed in Canada on alkaline paper

Contents

FROM *A Dream of Maps* (1981)

Last Supper 11

FROM *A Round House* (1983)

View from a Hammock 12
The Shoplifter 13
Singing Class 14
Captain Marsh 15
Preparation for Survival 16
No Head 17
Imagined Arrival 18

FROM *The Lame Waltzer* (1985)

Ends 19
Watches 20
The Applicants 21
Simultaneous Stories 22
Relics 23
The Boys in the Backroom 24
Cuba Street 25
A Scriptwriter's Discipline 26
The Submerged Door 27

FROM *Blue Shoes* (1989)

The U-Boat 28
A Couple Waiting 29
The Shadow Home 30
A Daydream Ahead 31
The Crab Rock 33
Where Fishermen Can't Swim 34
On My Own 35

A Postcard of a Hanging 36
Symmetry 37
Pink Milk 38
The Colour of Telephones 39
The Women 40
Flying Machines 41
To the Building Trade 42
Tube Ride to Martha's 43
Blue Shoes 44

FROM *The Flying Spring Onion* (1992)

Gold 46
The Money Tree 47

FROM *Cacti* (1992)

Sugar 49
A Peculiar Suicide 50
The Eagle 51
His Dog 52
The Aunt I Never Met 53
Biscuit Men 54
Cacti 55
His Dreams 56
Hanging 57
Digging 58
Surplus Light 59
The Desert 60
Artificial Blood 61
Melon Days 62
The Aviary 63
New Rules 65
The Blind Men 66
Asleep in a Chair 67
Monkey 68

After Closing Time 69
Donegal, Arizona 70

FROM *Fatso in the Red Suit* (1996)

A Boy 71
Bones 72

FROM *The Bridal Suite* (1997)

Reconfirming Light 73
Princess 74
Try Biting 75
In a Field 76
The Glass Coffin 77
The Bells 78
The House 79
The Box 80
Poker 81
Upstairs 82
The Sea 83
The Hat 84
Bagpipes 85
The Wobble 86
Goodbye to the Sky 87
Never in Life 89
The Bridal Suite 90
Reading 91
Crossing 92
Initiation 93
Donkey Hoof 94
The Compromise 95
Russian 96
Postcards 97
An End 98
The Blue Taps 99

The Butcher 100
Elm 101
Skating 102
The Bat 103
A Picnic on Ice 104

FROM *Up on the Roof* (2001)

Ghost Story 105
Up on the Roof 106

FROM *A Smell of Fish* (2000)

The Tunnel 108
The Tombs 109
The Lake 110
The Attic 112
Wading 114
The Flies 115
The Appointment 116
The Volcano 118
Blue Train 119
France 120
Guardian of the Women's Loo in Waterloo 121
Long Distance 123
Our Resident 124
The Houseboat 126
The Zookeeper's Troubles 127
Animals 128
Roadkill 129
A Smell of Fish 130
The Moths 131
Abandoned 132
Sipping Frascati in Castel Gandolfo 133
Do Not Throw Stones at This Sign 134
In the Ice 135

Incident in Exeter Station 138
Witness 139
Sea Dance 140
Swimmer 141
Sweeney 142

New Poems

Urine Therapy 143
Anniversary Choir 144
Frog-taming 146
Sanctuary 147

LAST SUPPER

It's a time for wild cooking.
A wind skims the Atlantic
so fierce it draws the future.
Cairns and transmitters shake on hilltops.
Rain reproduces the sea.

So call the butcher on the telephone,
halve his stock. Send the child
in a thick anorak up the garden.
Set the six gas-rings on at once.
Gather the herbs and go.

Beyond the pane, slates are falling.
The mail is late. But the water
piped from the reservoir on the horizon
is flowing freely. Enough
for six pots and more.

And the guests owed for years
can arrive with wine,
abandoning cars in the yard,
hats held tight with gloves
as they ring the bell,

then enter the vacuumed corridor
to lights dimmed, candles arrayed
on tables with Christmas silver.
And the odour adrift in the air
preceding the feast.

And the sound of Brahms, say,
drowning the wind. And the topics,
between mouthfuls, kept to the past:
religion's mercy, and Mass
in those days read in Latin.

VIEW FROM A HAMMOCK

for Padraig Rooney

It is stained with wine, moored to a tree.
Around it the garden groups: roses, a table,
vines that have strayed too far north.

It hangs there, mostly unused.
Winds come, attempt to swirl it off –
it, made of holes tied together?

Help it, place your body there.
Feet head-high, arms loose –
climb there, sway on that absent sea.

Night is the best time: the dark
attentive to the skin. Midges are gone.
Spiders patrol the grass.

Hear the head empty of sounds.
Swing the eyes in an arc, on a city of
leaves, shutters, moonlit shreds of sky.

THE SHOPLIFTER

The shoplifter has cut his hair
and bought a house by the sea.

His books come in useful now
as each time he has shinned

with an aerial up the chimney
Viking wind has ripped it down.

Outside the door, a black
mound of mussel shells has grown

near the fronds of marijuana
and carrots that thrive in the sandy soil.

He has learned the use of coins
for milk and beef, bakes daily

and lopes through the chill of daybreak
leaving footprints for the sea.

News is an old phenomenon.
Last year a bottle landed –

green, it sits on his mantelpiece.
He thinks it is Scandinavian.

SINGING CLASS

There is this image of a tuning-fork
struck against a desk-top to loose
its lone note into a draughty room.
Then the vocal summits of the class

with one boy at least in their midst
dumb for an hour, mouthing air
the song-words flitting through his head
his eyes never leaving the inspector.

CAPTAIN MARSH

Captain Marsh has gone to work
in a locked room on the second floor.
He is not pleased by steps approaching.

We are close enough. Listen, he types
with two fingers and barks at mistakes
as if at insolent cabin-boys.

All winter he is marooned here
by his own orders. An electric fire
and a whiskey-bottle are his comforts.

He has not spoken to us in months
though sometimes notes escape the room
requesting steak or lamb curry.

Nights when we can't sleep, we hear
the clacking of his machine far up
disturbing the pigeons on the rooftop.

What is his great vocation? When
will he reveal this late crop,
this surge that has replaced the sea?

We ask, make crude guesses, laugh.
Sometimes we wait outside the room
as he walks the boards as if in pain.

PREPARATION FOR SURVIVAL

for Philip Casey

Somewhere a man is swathed in furs
and is growing a beard of ice.
A survivor from an expedition
to set a flag at the absolute north
he chose to stay there
and learned to withstand cold.

He flies an aerial from the flagpole
and each month a plane leaves Greenland:
meat and coffee parachute down.
A temporary pleasure. The trade-
winds practise with pollen
above the submarines far south.

Audience at the war theatre,
fire will briefly light his sky
then a finite crackle on the radio.
Expert now in the disciplines of snow
he is learning to spear moose
or to fish through portholes in the ice.

NO HEAD

after an essay by D.E. Harding

I have no head,
no name, past or future.
To look is all.

Where my head should be
are houses, lampposts, traffic,
ivy, the bottom of sky.

Others have heads –
I watch you. But I have no head
and I see none like me.

And none of you stare
as I sit on a wall and air
flows over my torso.

Stopped, you laugh.
What's that, you say, on shoulders
with hair and green eyes?

You are wrong. Come closer
see half a man; closer still
a blur, then nothing.

I have no head. Those
in my mirror, eggspoon and hubcaps
are planted imposters.

Let them dare sit here
where I can dispute them. I breathe,
they dissolve in a mist.

IMAGINED ARRIVAL

White are the streets in this shabbiest-
grown of the world's great cities,
whiter than marshmallow angels.
Descending by parachute, one would be
arriving in a world long dead.
One would also be stiff with cold.

And if one, perhaps, would dangle there
in a skeletal tree, swigging brandy
from the equipment, rubbing fur ear-flaps,
one would have a view of the street
unhindered by involvement, as about one
the parachute would hang like snow.

And while getting one's wits back, groping
for a knife, a slow van would stop
leaving bottles of snow; and a man nearby
would dig the white from his steps
while a woman in a window opposite
might smile as he uncovered dirt.

By this stage pigeons would investigate
and one's toes would long be numb.
One would give up, and call for help
or if successful with the knife, drop down
leaving onlookers noticing the parachute
as one asked for soup and began to explain.

ENDS

At my end of the earth the Atlantic began.
On good days trawlers were flecks far out,
at night the green waves were luminous.
Gulls were the birds that gobbled my crusts
and the air in my bedroom was salty.
For two weeks once a whale decayed
on the pale beach while no one swam.
It was gelignite that cleared the air.

The uses of village carpenters were many.
Mine made me a pine box with a door,
tarpaulin-roofed, a front of fine-meshed wire.
It suited my friend, the albino mouse
who came from Derry and ate newspaper
and laid black grains on the floor.
When he walked his tail slithered behind.
And when I holidayed once, he starved.

WATCHES

He lifts a watch to his ear and listens,
all the time eyeing the Cherokee woman
stood alone at the bar with her gin
giving her own watch interrogations.
The barman behind her likes to whistle
twenties tunes, and has ten hands.
She has two, and like a miniature star
that dropped on the street to roll in
through the legs of the drinkers, up
her long thigh, over the purple cotton
to rest on her wrist, the watch glints –
must be echt silver or something,
and there she's glancing at it again
so he listens to his to help time go,
arching his brows at those cheekbones
and the blackest hair he has ever seen.

THE APPLICANTS

They were turned away with a shake of hands,
a shrug, a live butt landing on the street.
Away they went through the maze of Soho,
avoiding bananas fallen from barrows, or
the diabolical eyes of men in doorways.
A clock chimed but they forgot to count.

He suggested a cappuccino, she agreed.
Ducking, he held the door open for her,
they sat beneath an angled, concave mirror.
Her circling spoon made the most noise
as he stared at a puddle on the formica.
That clock chimed again before they left.

They made a bleak picture at the bus-stop,
huddled there, in an imaginary rain.
The bus slowed, she was first to board –
a pixy figure, all of four feet tall,
and, as the queue advanced with smiles,
he followed, crouched to miss the ceiling.

SIMULTANEOUS STORIES

There was the story of a power station
sinking into the very bog that fed it,
an inch or so a year, and still it burned
all the turf around it, so the hi-fis,
shavers, and vibrators could drone on
as near as upstairs, as far as the city.

And at the same time there was a hill
two of us climbed, earning our sleep,
to the wide, uncanny blue of the ocean
where a glimpse of Scotland bobbed.
Coming down, we found a ruined pram
from the 1950s, and spooked a hare
to skedaddle on up the promontory.

RELICS

The cleaver, hung on the scullery wall
these twenty years, gleamed once,
suffered the rasp of the backyard stone
to joint with ease the lambs he bought
on those monthly trips to Carn fair.
The basin that once caught lamb's blood
for black pudding, holds clothes-pegs
in the back bedroom where he slept
and on whose walls a holster hung
through my childhood, empty of its gun.
The backyard dancehall that he built
is a giant junkroom, with old papers
and coats, beds, prams, cans of paint.
The big house with poky rooms is flaking.
The mangle in the washhouse rolls
as it did for him, though the clothes
are machine-washed and spun dry.
The garden is a hedged-in field
where windfalls hide in the long grass.
The turkey stuffing alone survives
from his kitchen ways. The turfhouse walls
are rusted and patched with zinc,
and contain the hulk of the generator
by which, in advance of the government,
he brought electricity to the house.

THE BOYS IN THE BACKROOM

Lean on a wall and talk about gold –
a blinding, twelve-inch golden disc.
When they have it they will smash it
or melt it down to a yellow ball
to heave at a politician's window.

They will go on tour to Germany
and play a gig at the Reichstag
to a crowd as big as Hitler drew.
Airmen in wool-backed leather,
they will play through till dawn

amps throwing their chords
across the lake to the iron East,
their words about epidemics,
freeze-outs, global shutdown,
fighting the hum of patrol boats.

They will buy out a Highland laird ...
But their beer-break is over,
they flick their guitars alive,
take off behind the disused bar
and set the bare lightbulb dancing.

CUBA STREET

Midnight on the Isle of Dogs.
Taxis gather on Cuba Street
like roaches in a kitchen.
Black stockings, foxes round the neck
and grey stilettos ... They peer
through sodium fog at Rik's place.
Each has a passport of wine.
The throbs of a bass guitar
pass through them to the tankers
whose oil tints the water.
Purple bulbs down the stairs,
a woman's arm through the banisters
while a new friend fucks her ...
Someone yells from the bathroom
for a corkscrew, and they
continue their hunt for Rik.
They unearth him in the bedroom
holding court by his coffin,
the black one on four legs.
He is explaining relativity
with patience to an art-
college crowd, his centre parting
impeccable as a fish skeleton,
his red line of a tie unstained.
He yawns, climbs in his coffin
onto stitched red satin
and stretches his white toes.
'Would you be a doll,' he whispers
to a girl in a tubular dress,
'and screw the lid down.
And muffle that awful band.'

A SCRIPTWRITER'S DISCIPLINE

for Aidan Murphy

The last week in March the rains come.
I move indoors with two brown bags
of freezer fodder, a bottle of malt,
a score of beers, half a dozen clarets
and a new ribbon for my typewriter.
I use the wet to get things done.

For ten days the flat roof suffers
while underneath I fill a bucket
with olive stones, bacon rind and pages.
Deaf to the doorbell, I invent
lines for an Esperanto-learning cop
and his dumb, dope-smoking son.

There is a beauty in blank paper
as in a skilful TV silence
where the eyes' work is undistracted.
I have a cupboard full of videos
of silent movies, and Kojak
in colour with the soundtrack lost.

The studio knows not to phone me.
Curtained off, in my rocking chair,
not at home to Marconi or Baird,
I concoct fake lives, while
a forest of empties grows around me
and outside stray rivers course by.

THE SUBMERGED DOOR

The bridge by the chocolate shop
arcs like a rainbow whose hues
have drained to a pool of oil
motionless on the black water,
and a boy with a bicycle
dismounts here daily, climbs down
to the canal edge and kneels
peering into the water, moving
his gaze like a torch-beam
until it lights on the door,
and sometimes he reaches
through the oily wet to touch it,
sliding his fingers over panels
smooth from eels and water,
pausing at the letterbox,
and he imagines again the dawn-
crowd leaving the party,
taking the door with them,
laughing as it fell from the bridge,
floated, then slowly sank.

THE U-BOAT

I am floating by the wrecked U-boat,
naked as a dolphin in the August sun.
I've got away, again, from everyone.
I've moored my raft to the periscope
that stays underwater. On it I keep
my shorts and shoes, and Coca-Cola,
and a Bavarian girly magazine.
I've become so at-home in the ocean
that I think I must someday drown.
Miles away, on the edge of my hometown,
twin cooling towers fork the sky
where an airship phuts, selling beer.
No one knows the U-boat is here –
no boats approach these rocks,
no swimmers advance. I don't advertise.
I dive to the conning-tower and enter.
Bubbles speed behind me, above me,
but I am fast. I slide past my friend
the skeleton, until my breath runs low,
then I hit the surface he saw long ago
but never quite saw in the end.

A COUPLE WAITING

Leaving the door of the whitewashed house ajar
the man runs to the top of the hill
where he shields his eyes from the evening sun
and scans the sea. Behind him, a woman
holds a curtain back, but when he turns
and shakes his head, she lets the curtain fall.
She goes to the mirror beneath the flag
where she searches her face for signs of
the change her body tells her has begun.
The man shuts the door and sits at the table
where a chicken's bones are spread on two plates.
He thinks of his friends on the Atlantic,
coming up the western coast, laden
with well-wrapped bundles for his stable
that no horse uses. He thinks of his country,
and how his friends and he, with the help
of those bundles, would begin to set it right.
He calls the woman over and feels her stomach,
then asks why she thinks the boat is late.
Like him, she's harassed by an image –
the boat, searchlit, in French or Spanish waters,
guns pointed, a mouth at a megaphone.
Like him, she does not voice her mind,
instead sends him to the hill once more
in the dying light, to watch the red sun
sink in the water that's otherwise bare,
while she sits in the dark room, thinking
of the country their child will grow up in.

THE SHADOW HOME

As his daughter watches from the doorway
she can't realise how exactly
she has got him right – how each time
he carries his kitbag to the bus
he will end his journey at another house
where another daughter will wait for him.
And another wife will embrace him,
as her mother did just now,
and all three will go inside.
What she doesn't know, his daughter, is where –
some corner of Connecticut,
some Atlantic island – there are no leads,
and she would never ask.
And does her shadow-sister look like her?
Is she blonde, is her mother blonde,
do they speak English, has her father
hidden a language for years?
And does he take his other daughter
on long walks through the pines,
and tell her about his travels,
about the people he's met, about himself?
There is so much about her father
she does not know, and so little time
between his absences to learn it.
Does her shadow-sister know about her,
or does she begin to suspect?
Which of the two is the shadow home?

A DAYDREAM AHEAD

The car you bought
stays white that first spring,
or it does in my imagining
as I daydream ahead
and I am not there.

You step out
to a familiar petrol pump
(though new to me), plump
with the third child
you said you wanted.

The car is a make
I do not recognise
though I can tell by its size
how much you're earning
or your new man is.

Your hair is short
and it suits. You look good,
the few years have made
no difference.
You like life now.

Back in the car
you speed along a coast
that looks like the West
of Ireland.
You have gone home.

You come to a drive,
gravel sprays beneath you.
Your bungalow is new,

with portholes
and bay windows.

I sit at my window
whose net curtain blurs
a coloured line of cars
at parking-meters
beneath streetlights.

THE CRAB ROCK

Even in a bad summer the tide goes out
till the crab rock is revealed,
though the crabs like sun, like to climb there
and lie, as if dead, or lazily scuttle
among themselves, over weed and mussels.

Enough of their dead litter the beach
on the approach to the rock, waiting for water
to move them, out where no dog
or gull can poke them, where they'll dissolve.
They are back before the others know it.

The crab rock is never embedded in sand,
always those yards for us to wade through,
then the walk through edible claws
on bare edible toes. There are many crabs,
they are home, they are armoured.

I bet they leave when the sea covers,
though it's seldom deep there. A man could stand
all night and keep his head in air.
There are worse pastimes. Rain wouldn't matter.
The crabs would keep their distance.

WHERE FISHERMEN CAN'T SWIM

Back there where fishermen can't swim,
where the ice-age coast of Donegal
leaves rocks among the waves,
a lobster-boat cast off, whose engine
croaked before the rocks were by.
The youngest in the crew leapt out
onto a rock to push the boat away,
then laughed when he couldn't jump back.
But exactly when did he realise
that the boat would float no nearer;
that all those pulls on the engine cord
would yield no shudders; that no rope
or lifebelt existed to be thrown;
that those flares were lost in cloud;
that the radio would bring a copter
an hour later? He had forty minutes –
to cling while the waves attacked,
to feel the rock gradually submerge.
And they had forty minutes of watching,
shouting into the radio, till he cried
out, sank from view, and stayed there.

ON MY OWN

I stop, in my tracksuit, on a sleeper.
I lay my ear to the line
and if I hear a hum, slide
down the embankment, and wait
among the Coke-cans and beetles
till the express shakes by.
I think of last week, and McArdle
headless when the train had gone.
I scramble up to the tracks
that are blankly silver, and the sea
comes in view, and the young forest,
and the cross-country race I abandoned,
and my school's water tower – and I
head towards Dublin on my own.

A POSTCARD OF A HANGING

for Padraig Rooney

I sent you a postcard of a hanging,
the first one I attended, not thinking
I'd like it, or even stand it, as you
must have loathed my postcard too
till you realised it must be a trick,
a decadent, oriental gimmick
to put liberals off their breakfast
of an egg, toast, jam and the rest.

I imagine your laughs then, the card
propped against the milk, as you read
again how I thrived in the East –
every meal a ginger and chili feast;
the girls; the boys ...; how vibrant
the hours and how little I spent.
And you believed it, you knew
that all my varied antics were true.

And you turned to the picture again,
a colour print – a gallows, two men,
one hooded, one holding a noose
of whitest rope, for the moment loose,
and low in the foreground, a crowd
of men mainly, silently loud,
all Eastern, except for two or three –
one of whom, if you look closely, is me.

SYMMETRY

Gentlemen, you will please wear a tie
while peeing. And in the criss-cross corridors
you will pass without touching,
as you journey to and from the dining-room
under the portraits of Prime Ministers
(except for the woman). You will sit
equally spaced apart, four facing four,
with one (each of you in turn) facing me
down the long, driftwood table.
While eating, you needn't call me Sir.

Two legs of lamb must be carved
simultaneously. Decide among yourselves.
And eat as much or as little as you like
but eat the same. Your weights
must match at the end as at the start;
must be half of mine. And no glass
can go empty of blood-red wine
till the clock-hands cross at midnight
when I will retire. Leaving nine.
Gentlemen, you will please set that right.

PINK MILK

When the goats ate the red carnations
and the next morning's milk was pink,
the abbot loved it, demanded more

but the monks loved their flower-garden
and turned to cochineal, to crushed ants,
to paprika, all stirred in milk

to no avail – the perfume was gone
and the abbot grumpy, so carnations
were sacrificed to rampant goats

whose beards jigged as they chewed,
who looked up at the watching monks
while the abbot watched from a window

and in the kitchen, a leg of pork
thawed on a hook from the ceiling,
and blood dripped into a milk-jug.

THE COLOUR OF TELEPHONES

What colour is your telephone?
Is it blue, like mine –
blue in a blue-painted room
where the sun, at dawn,
comes down the stairs
from the roof-garden?
The colour is more important
than you may realise. Did you
send back a beige phone,
like I did, or is beige
your colour, your everyday?
After the maze of connection,
through subterranean tunnels,
via satellites,
it's essential to visualise
the person you speak to,
not just fix on a voice,
and the colour of the receiver
held to a mouth and ear
is a necessary detail,
as necessary as hairstyle.
You should give it to friends
when you give the number,
should keep it from strangers.
When you inherit a phone,
change the colour –
it's your personality, your secret,
a secret you should share.

THE WOMEN

The women are lighting fires
and snapping drunks –
their own drunks, men
whose eyes will be closed
on the prints that come back
from the chemist; men
seen past a whiskey bottle
on the table, drinking
from delft eggcups
beneath pictures of the dead.

The women are drinking too,
off-camera – till a child
grabs the camera
and snaps them, their laughs,
their glasses raised,
their mock dances to music
on the wireless; and the men
with their eggcups still,
deep in chairs, watching.
And the child wondering.

FLYING MACHINES

Waking to the sight of a windsock
on a deserted airfield, I inquire
and learn that men and women
jump from planes here, or loop
their loops, even into the ground.
I'm told that one rookie landed
on another taking off. I consider
Heathrow with my old fervour.
I travel by train to the west
where I'm brought on a windy walk
up a high path, among trees.
Far off, the Severn sprawls
as if it had no sea. And above me's
a glider, white and skull-frail,
audible above the wind! Skimming
the tree-tops metres from my head.
A model plane with someone inside.
And I think of the kits I bought
in Derry, then glued by numbers –
Spitfires, and Messerschmidts,
Hurricanes, and Stukas; the hours
I spent on these, and on thoughts
of landing in the local bay
in my own flying boat, ferrying
friends to the party on the island –
me, who needs brandy to walk
towards a smiling hostess
up the gangway of a DC 10.

TO THE BUILDING TRADE

Here's to the building trade,
to the renovations and facelifts,
the fake Victorian façades;
to the dust-muffled din
that stops on Sundays;
to the men that make it,
especially one from Dalston
who, after a pint or two
and a ploughman's, fell –
but the scaffolding stayed up
till the flats were clean.
Here's to the offduty cabbie
in the first-floor kitchen
who saw him splatter
on the pavement; to the mate
with the trowel, staring down,
his question unanswered;
to the rent increase
and the officer who set it.
Here's to the young widow
whose home's in this city
where migrant scaffolding,
wherever she moves,
will find her walls sometime.

TUBE RIDE TO MARTHA'S

Before the sirens started, he was late –
late for a dinner at his woman's,
but he'd managed to find a good Rioja
and an excellent excuse: his cat
had burned her tail in the toaster
(this was true) and he'd brought her
to the vet and back in a cab.
He thought about a third cab to Martha's
but funds were low, and the tube ride
was four stops, a half hour with the walks.
He had a thriller in his carrier-bag,
a Ross McDonald, long out of print,
which he opened on the escalator, wanting
it finished tonight. When the smoke came
he hardly noticed, till the black guard
tried to hustle everyone upstairs,
and trains rushed by, without stopping,
and people pushed and screamed.
As the smoke got thicker and blacker
with flames growing fast, he realised
it was over, almost before it had begun.

BLUE SHOES

I see that day's non-headlines, as he did
    though they're smoky now –
a prince at playschool, a brat's betrothal.
Some days they rob the gossip entries
    in lieu of disasters.
    They missed his later.

The weather inch reads more like Sicily
    than England. I see him
hurrying towards the train, his hand
raised to his eyes, the sunglasses at home.
    I have his notes here,
    the last of any consequence.

All the women, it seems, wore blue shoes
    in keeping with the morning.
He played with patterns, with omens
he deciphered later. That particular day
    it was blue shoes
    for want of any better.

I see him with a letter and Xeroxed map
    leaving the station.
He is sucking mints, perhaps hungover.
At the school gates he checks his flies.
    He goes in the office,
    is lost from sight.

Did they know the strain of these visits?
    Did the kids care?
It was a long day, but not outlandish.
In his honour they had lunch in a pub.
    On another day
    it would have relaxed him.

He was chauffeured to the train in the end,
    an overwound watch.
He queued at a phone, his heart chugging.
A woman was speaking, a man waiting –
    the woman, he wrote,
    wore blue shoes.

Hard for me in this library to imagine
    that home journey,
the mounting pain in his mind and chest,
the prison of that train in motion.
    All I know is
    he thought he was dead.

And got off at a suburban station
    to ride in an ambulance
through all the jams of South London
to nurses and a narrow bed with wheels
    and electric wires
    on feet, wrists and heart.

I am reading over his own description
    of that evening –
how later, at home, he imagined
he'd got away with it, and drank.
    He got away
    for the time being.

For years, even, but what does it matter –
    he never forgot
that day of the interrupted train,
the only time in his life, late sun
    and pretty women
    wearing blue shoes.

GOLD

The gold bars lie buried in the silt
and three skeletons lie guarding them,
three males, though the squid who sleeps
in the first skull couldn't say
and couldn't care less. To her
it is a cave, a domed cavern
she shares with no one. And who
could expect her to guess the plans
that had pulsed there, stalled,
till the ship reached Spain – expect her
to dream the face of the new wife
whose image had lodged there,
the image that faded with death?
The second skull lies yards away
from its long bones, and this one
is empty. But this one, too,
had taken in Spanish and spoken it out,
and had often eyed the gold.
Its eye-holes stare there still.
A crab sits in the third skull,
watching – a spider gone hard.
He is dictator of this stretch
of water, and the fact that he sits
in the skull of a Captain
is as useless to him as gold.
And nowhere on the skull wall
is a wisp of the knowledge
that the Captain's villa is ruined.
And the gold bars were going there
unknown to the crew. And unknown
to the divers whose boat churns above –
all they know is there's gold here.

THE MONEY TREE

Listen, there is a money tree.
I know you don't believe me,
and I didn't when Bill told me
that his mate Joe's brother
waters it every day.

It's not just water – there's sweat
and blood mixed in, not so's
you'd notice, Joe's brother says,
and he should know because
he mixes it himself.

There's another works with him,
another money-gardener
and they hate each other,
watch each other like dogs –
that's part of the job.

The tree is in a courtyard
surrounded by blank walls
with slits for rifles,
and a ceiling of perspex
that can slide open.

Where is this courtyard?
Joe's brother doesn't know.
Every morning he has to go
to a rooftop in the city
where a copter lands.

They put on a blindfold
and no one speaks. They whirr
Joe's brother somewhere

in the city, he can't say.
It's best he can't.

Why is there only one tree?
That's what I want to know.
You'd think they'd grow
plantations of the stuff.
Joe's brother laughs.

He sees the look
on the faces that come
every weekday at noon
to collect the picked leaves.
They wouldn't share.

If you still don't believe me
come here and we'll go
see Bill, and then Joe
and then his brother,
and ask him yourself.

SUGAR

From the high window he watches
his father's light plane
clear the mountain
and head for the rising sun.
He lies back on his bed
and thinks of sugar,
and the toffee he'll make
when his father gets back.
Next door he hears his mother
is up and dressed, and knows
she'll be in, opening curtains,
warning of breakfast,
and soon the smells of coffee
will drift upstairs
under his door,
coffee without sugar.
He imagines a line of ants
night after night
crossing the veranda,
each with a grain in its jaws.
He imagines keeping bees,
their sweetening hum
filling the garden
as he approaches
in his white armour.
He goes again to the window
where the usual gunfire
crackles beyond the river.

A PECULIAR SUICIDE

Begin with the note left on the table,
saying 'You'll never find me',
in a ring of photographs of sons.

Ask the moustached, diving policeman
how many river-holes he searched
where the salmon spawn in glaur.

Ask his colleagues, ask the long one
who searched the farm – he'll tell you
he found nothing bar the note.

Ask the neighbour who played dominoes,
as usual, with him in the bar
the night before he disappeared,

and who saw the spade was missing
from its usual place, and got
the assembled police wondering why.

Got them scouring the grassland
around the house, until finally
they found it, and freshly laid sods

hiding planks and a bin-lid
with a rope attached, and a tunnel
that didn't go very far.

Ask what they found at the end –
just him, and the pill jar,
and the coldest hot-water bottle of all.

THE EAGLE

My father is writing in Irish.
The English language, with all its facts
will not do. It is too modern.
It is good for plane-crashes, for unemployment,
but not for the unexplained return
of the eagle to Donegal.

He describes the settled pair
in their eyrie on the not-so-high mountain.
He uses an archaic Irish
to describe what used to be, what is again,
though hunters are reluctant
to agree on what will be.

He's coined a new word
for vigilantes who keep a camera watch
on the foothills. He joins them
when he's not writing, and when he is.
He writes about giant eggs,
about a whole new strain.

He brings in folklore
and folk-prophecy. He brings in the date
when the last golden eagle
was glimpsed there. The research is new
and dodgy, but the praise
is as old as the eagle.

HIS DOG

Where is this dog he sees and I can't?
Why is he pointing to the window,
then beckoning me to rise from bed
and herd his sheep back to the hills?
All around me sick men sleep through
his hissed commands, his tearing cries
that the night-nurse runs to calm –

a calm that night-lights can't prolong,
or daylight either, though his daughters
when they come with wills that lack
his signature, don't get a sound
or a move from him, don't get the farm,
although they plead and squabble.
Where is his dog now, where is it?

THE AUNT I NEVER MET

The aunt I never met was black-haired
and holy. She sang in the choir
on Sundays. She also helped
my grandfather butcher the lambs
he kept in the long grass at the back –
even he agreed she was the best
with the cleaver. She played tennis
with priests, and beat them,
and drank Bloody Marys from a bottle
during whist drives, and owned
the only yellow bubblecar in Ulster
(now in a private collection
in Guernsey). During the war
she took up German, crossed her sevens,
lit the odd bonfire at night
on the cliff edge, and did no good.
French toast and salmon were her favourites.
She hated kids – her eventual undoing,
if you ask me. Why else did she
end her days in that old farmhouse
hidden by trees, where the outside light
stayed on all night to lure
visitors, even family, who never came?
Why else did I never meet her?

BISCUIT MEN

Making biscuits shaped like men,
baking them until they're brown,
eating all the heads, and then ...
He always got stuck here, as though
he was one of the biscuit men,
and the cardboard woman he imagined
singing the nursery rhyme
in the piny kitchen was standing
by his elbow in the study
where he went every day to try
to get past these rhymes,
to bleed them out of his head.

But they wouldn't go, and she
was down on the street again,
beneath his window, bags at her feet,
while a cabbie braked,
then reached up to switch off
his yellow light, as she got in
without a glance up at him
where he'd stand for hours.
... dumping them into the bin ...
Dumping one ... He still had a head
that was full of nursery rhymes
or bits, and she was their star.

CACTI

After she left he bought another cactus
just like the one she'd bought him
in the airport in Marrakesh. He had to hunt
through London, and then, in Camden,
among hordes of hand-holding kids
who clog the market, he found it,
bought it, and brought it home to hers.
Next week he was back for another,
then another. He was coaxed into trying
different breeds, bright ones flashing red –
like the smile of the shop-girl
he hadn't noticed. He bought a rug, too,
sand-coloured, for the living-room,
and spent a weekend repainting
the walls beige, the ceiling pale blue.
He had the worn, black suite re-upholstered
in tan, and took to lying on the sofa
in a brown djellaba, with the cacti all around,
and Arab music on. If she should come back,
he thought, she might feel at home.

HIS DREAMS

He dreamed he was found on the sofa
saturated with his own blood.
He dreamed his daughter picked her nose
as she walked behind the coffin.
He dreamed the date of his death
and re-dreamed it the next night.
He ran to his homoeopathic doctor.

He took his pills and drops to bed
and didn't dream the first night.
Or did he, was that mood a dream
half-forgotten? The night after
he dreamed his wife's head
sawn in half down the nose,
the profiles mouth to mouth, in a kiss.

HANGING

Hanging from the lamppost
he could see far –
cars parked to the street's end,
the few late-night walkers
most of whom ignored him
hanging there. He could hear
screams and running feet,
also quick shuffles away
and, eventually, the wah-wahs
that came with blue lights
that led in the dawn.
Then the lights in all the houses
went on, and dressing-gown
wearers gathered, killing yawns.
And flashbulbs exploded,
though he couldn't hold
his head up, and his face
was blue. A megaphone
asked the crowd to go home
as a ladder leant on the lamppost
for someone to ascend.
He looked into this man's eye
as the knife cut him down.

DIGGING

Out in the park two children are digging,
two girls, their long hair wind-tossed and free.
They are making little headway
although they lean with all their might.
Someone ought to tell them their flat shovel
is not the tool. Someone ought to take
that blown-off branch still sprouting leaves
that lies on the ground by their feet
and start a bonfire with it, let loose
its green smoke. Someone ought to say
it's too frail and long to plant,
too late to set. But the two girls keep digging,
with the mother-trunk firm above them,
and behind, the one lamp in the street still on.

SURPLUS LIGHT

Could be the making of your marriage,
or of your divorce. Try it at dusk,
when it comes into its own. Sit there
at my window with the curtains open,
as daylight shrinks behind silhouettes
of buildings like my own. See how
its headstart leaves the others standing
(which, of course, they are), even though
one hour later they're a staggered line
of lit streetlights on a night street.

Hard for you, I expect, to imagine
the effect on the nerves of witnessing
such relentless light, of seeing it
take on the sun and wear it down.
That's apart from its unlikely beauty –
my iron star-tree I could call it
but I won't. And to think that I rang
the Council to complain! What are rates
compared to this gift of surplus light,
this permanent reminder of wastage?

THE DESERT

He wanted rim-bel-terfass and nothing else.
He wanted a space-shot of the desert.
He wanted that Algerian woman he'd known
years before, who'd fed him couscous,
with rosewater made by her own mother.
He'd had a male friend who taught there,
on an oasis – he wanted him back there,
arriving, in the small hours, once a year
with dates, and goat-cheese, and the strong
red wines that held their own in France.
He wanted to be able to visit him –
take the train from Algiers, a rucksack
with bacon and whiskey on his back,
no advance warning, no Arabic, no French –
and send a series of postcards to himself
till, one by one, they all arrived back.

rim-bel-terfass: a stew made of gazelle meat, with Saharan truffles (Sahara dish)
                    –Larousse Gastronomique

ARTIFICIAL BLOOD

As the artificial blood that saved him
was Japanese, he went to live in Japan.
And of course he found the raw fish
the best for his patched-up heart.
The doctors were reassuring too,
even if they spoke a stretched English
and couldn't laugh. He kept in touch
with his golfer son – golf was played
throughout Japan; perhaps one day
his son would visit with saké ...
Some nights he'd walk to a noodle bar
and point, then eat. He'd hurry
past the geisha parlours, and maybe
he'd stop at a phone, then stay outside
till he was too tired to remember
those walks on the Malvern Hills
he'd taken too seldom, too long ago
when his son was little, his wife alive,
before his heart operation,
before the white, thin artificial blood
entered his body and led him to Japan.

MELON DAYS

That autumn the newspapers were numbing.
Even the books he read kept him awake,
applying the written lives to his own,
trying on the deaths. And when friends called
with facts of the deaths of fathers
he had already decided that sporadic
melon days were needed, whole days
where he'd eat only melons, and keep
his vital sacs and tracts in shape.
So he brought bags to the nearby market
and filled them with melons, after pressing
for ripeness and sniffing for taste,
and as he waited to pay on that first day
he heard a fat man vow to lose weight
yet carry on eating a hamburger.
'Melon days,' he muttered, 'that's what you need.
Melon weeks. Melon years.' But the girl
who gave him change stared at him
and shook her head as he walked away.

THE AVIARY

Isn't it wild that Mary
abandoned the aviary
and went to Jamaica?
Can't you see her there,
with birds nowhere,
only black boys?
Can't you hear the sea
and smell the coffee
overlaid with ganja?
Isn't that a buzzard
on the postcard
she's sending home?
Wasn't it five years
she spent with the birds
that bugged her?
Or was it the bars
and not the birds
she railed at?
All that wire
caging the air
for cameras.
All those feathers,
in all weathers,
to clean up.
Look at Mary now,
look at how
brown she's become.
Listen to her laugh,
isn't it rough
on the poor girl.
Imagine, she *flew*
from Heathrow
to be there.

Let's send Mary
a baby canary
with clipped wings.
Let's remind Mary
of the aviary,
let's wish her well.

NEW RULES

Even his dog ran with a limp,
following his lopsided run
along the path by the River Wye
where cyclists came up behind,
ringing their tinny bells, shouting
when the dog wouldn't limp aside,
and the man wouldn't either.

And you had to agree with them,
the lame dog and the lame man.
Even to get into a tracksuit lame
is admirable. But to go running,
or what passed for it, and to buy
a lame dog, or lame a good dog –
that's when you're talking new rules.

THE BLIND MEN

They want it back, the blind men,
students of magnified touch,
evictees from this dingy house
whose bare walls they know by heart.
They want back in, and me out.
They still have keys they use
at night, to let me know –
by black hairs in the bath,
by a white stick under the stairs,
by tapping on bedroom doors
then not being there – that they
are the rightful tenants here,
and I've got to go. So I keep
the radio on, no television.
I stand in the mirrorless bathroom
and shave by touch, shivering
from the linoless floor. I cook
in the half-dark, and rarely work.
I keep my books hidden.
It's not as if it's a mansion –
the basement flooded last year,
as they will know, and the attic-
ladder's kaput – it's nowhere
to throw a party in, even if
people could find the street,
but they want it back, the blind men,
and they're not getting me out.

ASLEEP IN A CHAIR

Asleep in a chair for three hours?
Take that man away. Bind him
and bundle him into a mini-cab,
drive through the Southern English night
till you see the lights of Brighton,
then throw him out on the South Downs.

Hopefully it will be sub zero
and wet as Ireland. (*Drunk* and
asleep in a chair for three hours,
with the TV and the gas fire on?)
Pick a field with cattle in it,
or better still, a nervy horse.

Make sure there's no stream near,
or even a house. Get miles away
from a shop or a chemist –
empty out his pockets just in case.
Smash his glasses while you're at it.
Forget you liked him, lose his name.

Burn his shoes to ash beside him,
keep his jeans as a souvenir.
Cut his hair off (all his hair).
Asleep in a chair for three hours?
By the time you're finished, honey,
he might have learned to sleep in a bed.

MONKEY

Even when the monkey died
they never invited us round
to eat green banana curry
and play braille Scrabble
in that room underground
where twin hammocks hung
near the dead monkey's cage
that held him still, stuffed
and gutted, body-shampooed,
face locked in a rage
that quick death provides.
And none of us knew
what went on at the end,
whether poison, or heart,
or if one of them blew
their monkey away,
then turned on the other
and aimed that Luger,
that well-oiled Luger
at the brain of a brother,
but flung the gun down.
And with their excuse gone
we expected invites,
one big wake, perhaps,
complete with champagne,
and Joe, the taxidermist,
waiving his bill –
his grief-contribution,
his goody for the party.
We're all waiting still.

AFTER CLOSING TIME

> *'Those who don't believe in life after death should be here after closing time.'*
> – Notice inside an office in Derry's city cemetery.

The gate will be open, and streetlights
will guide you through the graves,
but you'd better watch your carry-outs
as the dead are barred from pubs.
Watch for the flowers that fly
from grave to grave, creating letters
for the papers and maybe more dead –
and one thing you'll know in the half-light
is that the dead are too many
to fit in the ground, too lively
to lie in a box, so they do
what you'd expect them to, and that's why
they surround you as you swig
from a can. They ruffle your hair,
breathe through unbrushed teeth,
fart even, and one of the pushier
puts his finger in the hole in his head
then invites you to follow. Another
opens his rotting shirt to show you
his two hearts, the old and the new,
and a one-legged ex-pensioner
eyes the bulge of your cigarettes,
and you'd be well advised to drain
one can, then chuck the other
as far as you're able, for the dead
hate those who outlive them,
and you'd be canny to suss this
and run, and hope the gate's not shut.

DONEGAL, ARIZONA

for Dermot Seymour

He put Donegal in the oven,
cooked it awhile, and got Arizona.
And he siphoned all that rain
and the troublesome Atlantic
into waterholes in the desert
and the Colorado River.
A few tons of gelignite
moved the hills together
to make the Grand Canyon,
and he stretched all the toads
to make Gila monsters,
and bought a few steamboats,
and buried gold in the hills.
The Indians were difficult
but he advertised abroad,
then the Mexican ambassador
signed the Treaty of Guadalupe
all over again, and Derry
stared at Sligo over a void.

A BOY

Half a mile from the sea,
in a house with a dozen bedrooms
he grew up. Who was he?
Oh, nobody much. A boy
with the usual likes
and more than a few dislikes.
Did he swim much? Nah,
that sea was the Atlantic
and out there is *Ice*land.
He kept his play inland
on an L-shaped football pitch
between the garage and the gate.
What did he eat?
Stuff his grandfather made,
home-made sausages,
potted pig's head.
He got the library keys
and carried eight books at a time
home, and he read.
He read so much
he stayed in the book's world.
Wind rattled the window
of his third-storey room,
but his bed was warm.
And he stayed in his bed
half the day if he could,
reading by candlelight
when the storms struck
and the electricity died.
How do I know all this?
You'd guess how if you tried.

BONES

The horse fell in the harbour,
was splashing in the water
with the cart strapped to his back.
And a cyclist with sunglasses
and a woman with a pram
kept on going – but not the man
with the mongrel in a sack.
He dropped all and dived straight in.

The horse kept neighing
while the man was saving him
and the dog was chewing free.
Maybe the horse knew
that the man was on his way
to drown the dog. Maybe the dog
had barked this to the horse.
Oh, there were bones in the cart.

RECONFIRMING LIGHT

for Tom Lynch

On Mullett Lake in mid-March
two pickups are parked by blue ice-shanties.
Fishermen are inside. Perch
and walleye are what they're after
through their holes in the ice, although
a week, two weeks from now is best,
right before the ice melts and thermal
inversion sends the fish wild.
And shanties and pickups go under.

Down there, deep, cruise the sturgeon,
big as torpedos. They're never seen
except when they lounge on the top
to reconfirm light, or when a hook
snags one and a boat's tugged in circles.
Slowly though. There are worse catches –
corpses that lie on the bottom all winter
then float up to be towed in,
wearing clothes a size too small for them.

PRINCESS

The boy who lives in the wrecked bus
down on the rocks, near the point
knows every yard of the long beach
that curves to the ruined castle
where the girl's skeleton lies
behind a wall – a false wall
that only the boy's discovered,
and only he knows the loose stones
that lift out to let him in,
so he can comb the long red hair
that's still attached to the skull,
and he brings her what he's found
that day on the beach, and calls her
what she was, Princess, even when
they walled her up in her room
and left her to die, alone
until the boy found her, and now
she's visited every day, and lies
surrounded by buoys, lifejackets,
lobster-floats, two odd shoes
(one with a bony foot still in it),
half of an oar, a rubber dingy
and a driftwood sculpture the boy made
on the day he guessed was her birthday
because of the rainbow he saw
ending at the castle, as he left the bus
and ran the three miles to her,
and the rainbow went as he got there.

TRY BITING

'Try biting,' said the sailor
to the man he'd tied up,
after punching out his teeth,
and pocketing his wallet,
and pulling on his jeans.
'Where's your passport, shit?
You've left it at home!'
So he kicked him again,
and when the man cried out
he kicked him again.
Then he gagged him
with the bloodstained shirt,
and when a dog came nosing
it got kicked, too,
and scurried, yelping,
out of the alleyway.
And the sailor laughed,
then tightened his belt,
before spitting on the man
and heading into town.
He'd have a few good ones,
he thought, beers first,
then whiskey. And a woman.
He stopped beneath a streetlight
to admire his jeans,
then turned to a window
to tidy his hair, and grin –
a wide, ivoried grin.

IN A FIELD

A shoelace and a penis lying in a field
on a cold, blue, February morning.
Is it hours, or days the police will take to find them?
And the shoes, the other lace, the rest of the man –
where are they in the crisp sunshine
(Conrad's favourite weather) while seagulls
cruise at sixty feet, at the furthest they've been inland
and a mouse, with eyes on the sky, sniffs the penis,
scurries away, along tyre-tracks,
through stubble, weaving, darting.
Which of the five murders, all with missing bodies,
that compete with Maastricht for the headlines,
is this fine one? Does anyone
know yet the penis is gone?
When the farmer, taking a shortcut home,
comes across it will he know what it is?
Will he pick it up in a hanky
and accelerate to the police?
And they, will they have a clue who it belongs to?
After poking at it, and peering at it, and scratching
and laughing, will they freeze it
till later, till they find bodies to check,
till a widow comes shaking and sobbing
and the penis and the rest of the body
go into the ground, or into fire together,
and slowly become forgotten?

THE GLASS COFFIN

The Brocagh boys
are carrying one of their number
in a glass coffin.
They are taking him
to his caravan, the best place
to wake him in.
They can see him
lying on his left side
facing the mountain.
One is pushing
his antiquated bicycle
behind the coffin.
They will go in the grave together,
first the bicycle,
then the glass coffin.
His third nervous breakdown
was his last one.
He won't ask again
how to spell three.
He won't fall in a sheugh
when he's in the grave.
The Brocagh girls
are leaving the factory
to wake him.
They are shouting
about nylons, for the legs,
for the thighs.
Some have bottles,
some have tyres
for a funeral blaze.
They follow the glass coffin
and the boys
up the steps of the caravan.

THE BELLS

for John Hartley Williams

Fighting the undertow,
watching the boat drift away,
the monk felt his habit grow
heavy as a suit of armour,
and struggled till he was naked,
hoping his fat would keep him
alive in the ice-berged Atlantic
until he caught the toe of rock
that kicked the sea to Ireland.
He clung to a plastic lunchbox
and thought of the veal pies
famous in the monastery, hoping
his surfeit years were enough
to keep him awake for five hours.
He thought of his antics
with the boy, behind the shed
where his boat was kept
waiting for today. He felt
his fingers get pins and needles
and his testicles go numb,
his feet become bare bone
and his eyes start to close.
He was so tired now,
already he heard the bells ring
in the distant fog. If he slept
he'd float there, in time for Mass.

THE HOUSE

The house had a dozen bedrooms,
each of them cold, and the wind
battered the windows and blew down
power-lines to leave the house dark.
Rats lived in the foundations,
sending scouts under the stairs
for a year or two, and once
a friendly ghost was glimpsed
at the foot of a bed. Downhill
half a mile was the Atlantic,
with its ration of the drowned –
one of whom visited the house,
carried there on a door.
It hosted dry corpses, too,
with nostrils huge to a child,
but never a murder –
except the lambs bled dry
in the yard outside. Sunlight
never took over the interior,
and after dark the cockroaches
came from under a cupboard
to be eaten by the dog.
Crows were always sitting
on the wires, planning nests
in the chimneys, and a shotgun
sometimes blew a few away.
Neighbours never entered
as often as in other houses,
but it did have a piano upstairs.
And I did grow up there.

THE BOX

79 years in a cast-iron box
in the basement of an old hotel
that was once the best in Donegal –
and only the porter could open the lock
to reveal what was in the box
and you wouldn't have guessed for a gillion
that a broken-up skeleton was in there
holding its skull in its hands,
with its legs folded beneath it,
and in the box alongside it
a yellowy scroll of pig's leather
sound as the day it was tanned.

It fell to the hotel manager
to read the scroll. A throat-clearing,
then a voice: *Here sits folded
Magnus McLaughlin, who did
more skitterish deeds in his life
than an English blackguard,
and so I built this box myself
to keep him in, and I chopped him
with the cleaver I kept for pork
and you should have seen the blood.*
She paused, and added *March 1913*.
And we all stared at the box.

POKER

There were five of us playing that night,
Padge, Kieran, Neal and me –
and, stretched out in his coffin, Uncle Charlie.
We dealt him a hand each time
and took it in turns to bet for him,
waiving his losses, pooling his wins,
for what good were coins to him?
What could he win but his life?
Still, five of us played that night
and when we stopped it was daylight.
We left the cards with him
to remind him, forever, of that game
and Padge, Kieran, Neal and me
went up the road to our beds
and slept until we buried him,
then played until we had to agree
the good hands had gone with Uncle Charlie.

UPSTAIRS

Last year I was going downstairs,
now I'm going upstairs. Up there
is a rocking horse in red velvet.
I'll dust him off with a crow's wing,
then I'll shake the kitchen ceiling.
I'll jump off in mid-buck, onto
the round water-bed I bounced on
with black-haired, patchouli-scented X
to the drawl of Mick Jagger.
I'll take the brass telescope to the window
to see if Mrs Voss is still undressing
with the blind drawn to her neck.
I'll fit together the owl-kite
and, opening the window, I'll feed
the kite to the sea wind,
wondering if it'll reach Iceland.
I'll rummage under the newspapers
till I find the carpenter's set
my Grandpa bought me, the saw
just right for severing flex.
I'll take a swig from the hip-flask,
then, locking the door, I'll switch
the light on, and I'll start sawing
three inches above the bulb.

THE SEA

Sitting on an upturned boat
in the green middle of a roundabout
overlooked by towers and crenellations,
she watched the cars curve by
and waited. Overhead, the gulls
kaokaoed the blue of the sky
where fat clouds floated, and a lone bee
was higher than ever before.
She looked at her handbag watch
just as a truckdriver hooted.
She glanced towards Aberdeen.
She felt the keys in her bag
and thought of the house on the island
where six years ago she'd eaten
an omelette of twelve quails' eggs
washed down with Chablis.
She'd hardly get there tonight.
Old pictures assaulted her,
floated in the haze – memories of
twenty or more black sheep
in a field that stopped at the sea.
And hundreds of gulls spread out
behind a ploughing tractor.
And a herd of lying-down cows.
And a cemetery in a golf course
that bordered the sea. All these
were waiting, but she was stuck
in the green middle of the roundabout,
sitting on the upturned boat,
and the sea stayed where it was.

THE HAT

A green hat is blowing through Harvard Square
and no one is trying to catch it.
Whoever has lost it has given up –
perhaps, because his wife was cheating,
he took it off and threw it like a frisbee,
trying to decapitate a statue
of a woman in her middle years
who doesn't look anything like his wife.
This wind wouldn't lift the hat alone,
and any man would be glad to keep it.
I can imagine – as it tumbles along,
gusting past cars, people, lampposts –
it sitting above a dark green suit.
The face between them would be bearded
and not unhealthy, yet. The eyes
would be green, too – an all-green man
thinking of his wife in another bed,
these thoughts all through the green hat,
like garlic in the pores, and no one,
no one pouncing on the hat to put it on.

BAGPIPES

The bagpipes on the wall began to skirl
the minute she reversed out the drive.
She took with her nothing but her spaniel
and the walnut clock, but they were enough
to convince him she was gone for good.
He stood watching as she swerved away,
out towards the sheep-encrusted headland
where she'd sat every day and painted
portraits of the waves, but today he knew
she wouldn't stop there, was only going
to skid a goodbye, before booting it south
to somewhere he wouldn't be. The bagpipes
droned on, needing no mouth to rouse them.
There was more than one set, clearly –
he'd gatecrashed a bagpipers' convention
in his own home, that was no home now.
He started to scream his accompaniment.
He threw a few mugs at the wall
and took the poker to the mirror.
Beneath it, the voodoo mask was laughing
like he always knew it would. She'd bought it.
She would never take that with her.
He looked at it, and ran at the window.
The bagpipes drowned out the breaking glass.

THE WOBBLE

Halfway across the ravine,
watched by more than a thousand
and a further million on TV,
he wobbled and almost fell.
Maybe the gasp held him up,
righted the wheel of his unicycle,
gave his legs a surge
that powered him across.
As the crowd hauled him off
and carried him aloft,
he thought of the wobble,
how it had tried to send him
down onto the steer-bones
at the ravine's bottom,
his cry echoing out over
the cries of the thousand,
till it suddenly cut off –
and he asked those carrying him
to return him to the ravine,
to his rope, still strung there,
and he took the unicycle,
turned the pedals and sent it
back where it had come from,
alone this time, the crowd quiet,
until halfway across, it fell
with a clatter and a cloud of dust.

GOODBYE TO THE SKY

i.m. Michelle

Let me tell you a story you'd have liked –
a small plane gets in trouble,
has to come down on a Devon road
and when it bumps to a halt
one wing is over a hedge, the other
sticks skewways into the path of cars,
and the young pilot walks away.
But he wouldn't have known he would,
when the instruments were saying
goodbye to the sky. I hear him
shouting to his wife, his children,
praying for the first time in years,
cursing, even, calling the plane
all kinds of jerry-built junk,
wishing he hadn't been bought
Airfix planes and Biggles books,
remembering his first tonguey kiss
and the last, that morning,
his lovely wife half-asleep
but turning to him, as if continuing
a dream he was happy to share,
unlike this daylit nightmare,
the terrible ground coming closer,
the road a parody of a runway
sandwiched between hedges,
and finally the jolt of the landing,
the best and the worst he'll ever do.
He walked away, that young man,
but you didn't, and your falling
lasted years. Hear this, though –
sticking into that same Devon sky

is a black obelisk, built to remember
the Waterloo dead, its inscription
Peace to the souls of the heroes
and hear it updated, in the singular.

NEVER IN LIFE

For eight days the sea held him,
or what was left of him,
for eight days the sea moved him about
through miles of underwater,
far from land, then close again,
till it left him afloat on his back
at the base of a cliff.

Before that, seals had circled
above where he'd settled,
alerting a Christian Brother diver
who hadn't gone deep enough
into the submerged wrack.

Two more had been with him
in the storm-tossed boat,
but they were waked already,
were stuck in blessed ground.
He had been given up
until the sheep boy saw him.

Never in life had he drawn a crowd
like the one spread out
along the clifftop, to witness
a door being dropped on ropes
then raised again with him tied on,
before being carried by six men
at the head of a procession,
a mile uphill to an ex-dancehall
which was ours.

THE BRIDAL SUITE

for Nuala Ní Dhomnaill

On the third night in the bridal suite
without the bride, he panicked.
He couldn't handle another dream like that,
not wet, like he'd expected,
but not dry either– men digging holes
that they'd fill with water, donkeys
crossing valleys that suddenly flooded.
The alarm-call had a job to wake him,
to send him out from the huge bed,
past the corner kissing-sofa, up two steps
to the shower he hardly needed,
where he'd scrub himself clean as the baby
he'd hoped to start that night,
under the canopy like a wimple,
in that room of pinks and greens.
Naked and dripping, he'd rung Reception
to see if she'd rung, then he'd stood
looking out at the new marina,
as if he'd glimpse her on a yacht.
On the third night he could take no more –
he dressed, to the smell of her perfume,
and leaving her clothes there,
the wedding dress in a pile in the wardrobe,
he walked past the deaf night porter,
out to his car. He had no idea
where he was headed, only that she,
if she ever came back, could sample
the bridal suite on her own,
could toss in that canopied bed
and tell him about her dreams.

READING

Yes, I was reading on the M1.
Yes, I was driving, and reading, too –
a book of poems by Paul Durcan,
The *Berlin Wall Café*, left by my wife
when she walked out. It wasn't
a twisty clifftop road I was reading on,
it was a motorway, and anybody
with one good eye in their head
could drive on that. Didn't I,
as a hitchhiking student, get asked
to drive a car for thirty miles
while the driver slept in the back?
I can't drive, I remember saying.
It's a motorway, he said. Just keep
in the slow lane, and bring her in
at the second next services.
And it wasn't a novel I was reading –
the thing about poems, Your Honour,
is they're mostly short. you can look up
between them, or between stanzas,
and see what's happening ahead.
Would you prefer if I'd been swigging
from a hip-flask, or sucking on a joint,
or canoodling ... ? Never mind that.
And what about that blind driver
whose dog barked at red lights?
I refute the charge of swaying
from lane to lane. I stayed in
the slow lane, did a steady 65.
It was 3 a.m., Your Honour, the motorway
was as quiet as it ever gets,
I had no one to hurry home to,
so I took out my Durcan and opened it.
It didn't seem a wrong thing at all!

CROSSING

He rode his horse into the sea and kept heeling it on.
The horse wasn't used to this, but proceeded to swim –
not easy, with the man and those wet jeans on its back –
but it made headway, out into the currents of the Channel
among the yachts, the windsurfers, the long-distance swimmers.
When the Caen to Portsmouth ferry passed, the Captain hooted.
The horse ignored this; the man took off his cap and waved.
Applause broke out among those few passengers on deck.
The man bowed his head into the sea and downed a mouthful.
He spat this out, then spoke for the first time to the horse
whose hooves kept flailing the water, swatting a few lobsters,
alarming squid, missing a frogman by centimetres.
The horse's head was higher now. Had it seen the Isle of Wight?
The man leant down and whispered promises in its ear –
once they hit land, a big bag of oats, a bigger bowl of cider.
He told it that no other horse had made this crossing,
and that once was enough – they'd take the ferry home.
The horse neighed as they passed a rock where a lighthouse
had just switched on, as if they both were expected,
and flashbulbs were ready on the beach, a studfarm waiting.

INITIATION

Out in the hills, the goat had been easy.
He'd creep up from behind, catch one horn
and enter her. She loved it, he knew,
so he thought he'd start pleasing women.

He stayed in the loo the whole way to London
and found a bedsit in Chelsea. Signed on,
took to hanging out in bars, chatted up
any woman he saw but bedded no one.

He went to museums that were free,
as he'd heard they were good for pick-ups.
He'd heard wrong. Still, the odd statue
had great breasts and he fondled them.

He became a reviewer of strip-shows.
He walked by the canal in the evenings,
keeping a lookout for sex in boats.
He bought a headband and a statue of Cupid.

He knew that soon he'd be overrun.
Meanwhile, he masturbated to a picture
of a woman masturbating, holding a mirror.
At least, this way he wouldn't need blood tests.

At last, he was picked up in his local
by a tall woman and a short one.
They took him home to their basement flat,
took turns with him and with each other.

It was different from the goat, he thought,
as the short woman coaxed him stiff
while the tall one tickled her with a feather.
Ah, the goat, he thought as he came in her mouth.

DONKEY HOOF

A donkey hoof makes the best brooch.
It also makes an excellent soup
and left in the sun, then crumbled,
it is the only true aphrodisiac.
Two donkey hooves mean luck at poker
but three mean a month in hospital,
and anything over three means death.

Ancient Egypt rubbed crushed hoof
into bald heads. I have no record
of its success, but I'm sure it worked.
All a Celtic cowherd needed
was a donkey hoof and donkey poem
and a young donkey was there to jump on.
A donkey hoof is the best currency.

Hollowed out, a hoof will float –
give one to your favourite toddler.
The lightest donkeys walk on water.
The world is crammed in a donkey hoof.
Petition NASA to blast one up
and loose it among the space debris.

THE COMPROMISE

He wanted to be buried on the moon.
At last he was answering the question
but she wouldn't have it. She laughed
and he laughed, but he persisted.
He brought it up at dinner parties.
He wrapped it in a joke, but she
knew he meant it. A guest said
there wouldn't be many at the funeral.
No maggots, though, another said,
and no graffiti on the gravestone,
at least for a decade or three.
She brought up the cost. He shrugged,
spoke of sponsorship, of ice-
preservation, of the enabling future.
He would be famous dead. A guest
proposed a grave on Iona, among
the graves of kings. Mentioned
that only twice had men landed
on the moon, and they were living.
Suggested writing to one. And asking
about grave-sites, she added.
He was undeflected. He repeated
he wanted to be buried on the moon,
whatever it took. He went quiet.
A fifth cork was popped, then he
offered a compromise, a heart-coffin
snug in the hold of a space-shuttle,
his heart in there, the rest of him
in Highgate, in Derry, in the sea.
They were all delighted to agree.

RUSSIAN

for Steve Regan

He woke up speaking Russian.
He lay there, amazed,
as sentence after sentence emerged
and sailed to the window –
it was verse, it had to be
to flow that rhythmically,
but he hadn't written it,
nor had he been to Russia.

His wife came in from church
to find pages of Cyrillic
on the bed, and her man
on the telephone, in Russian.
He was arguing, she knew that,
though about what?
When had he been to night class?
Was it him here at all?

She remembered the tapes
and his never-right French,
or that time in Prague
at the tram terminus
grasping for a phrase of Czech.
He had to be seriously sick
or possessed. In the pauses
she heard the answering Russian
faintly, a world away.

POSTCARDS

Sailed to Normandy in an afternoon haze,
peered out the window and drank some wine,
saw a dead gull floating on the Channel
and a piece of wood from a broken boat.
Thought of the postcards I could make of those,
how a market was there for cards of the dead –
planecrashes in Andean forests, hidden by leaves;
space-debris; the skeleton of a horse;
a wrecked tank in a Sarajevan suburb;
a pile of clothes left on an empty beach –
nothing as crude as a mutilated body.
I'd keep all my cards black and white
and limit them to a numbered hundred.
Yes, I could see them covering the wall
of the sitting room I'd hacked out of a cave
on the de-inhabited island I'd bought
with the proceeds of their sales. Around me
ruined crofts, rabbits zapped by myxomatosis,
a lighthouse that last shone in the 20s,
and the north wind blowing me to bone.

AN END

I want to end up on Inishtrahull,
in the small graveyard there
on the high side of the island,
carried there on a helicopter sling
with twenty speedboats following.
And I want my favourite Thai chef
flown there, a day before,
and brought to the local fishermen
so he can serve a chili feast
before we head off up the hill.
A bar, too, it goes without saying,
free to all, the beer icy,
the whiskey Irish, and loud
through speakers high on poles
the gruff voice of Tom Waits
causing the gulls to congregate.
Get Tom himself there if you can.
And in the box with me I want
a hipflask filled with Black Bush,
a pen and a blank notebook,
all the vitamins in one bottle,
my addressbook and ten pound coins.
Also, a Mandarin primer.
I want no flowers, only cacti
and my headstone must be glass.

THE BLUE TAPS

He left me the blue taps
from his blue bath.
He left me the cacti he spoke to.
I had to go and take them
from his grey house
before she sold it.
I had to stand there
in the blue living room
and ask her the names
he'd given all the cacti.
I had to leave her
with no taps in the bathroom.
She didn't seem to care.
I wanted to ask her
why he'd been blue-crazy,
or was she in it, too?
I wanted to know
how long they'd taken
to gather fifteen cacti,
and why he'd spoken to them.
I asked none of this,
just ferried my heirlooms
to the back seat of my car.
I hoped the taps fitted.
I hoped I could remember
the cacti's names
in the correct order.
I had a white bath,
but my living room was green.

THE BUTCHER

Most nights he climbs from the grave
and makes the trek to the village.
Rain washes the soil off, while the flesh
reconstitutes in the streetlight.
By the old dancehall he has clothes again
including the apron and a bloody cap.
He spits as he passes the supermarket
with its deep-freezes and cellophane.
He stares ahead as he passes the church,
then disappears into the betting shop.

It's then that the noise of the market-place
shuts out the noise of the track.
The ribbons of prize animals he'd bought,
the great hooks that held the joints,
the spike for the customers' accounts –
all these materialise around him
as he sets to sharpening the cleavers
and making the faggots and black pudding.
Already they are leaving the graveyard
and heading his way. They have until dawn.

ELM

Under the elm tree she died.
No one knew she'd gone there
that March afternoon, after
the botched paella, the white Rioja,
the cycle ride and the swim.
We were bunched around the hammock
taking turns to swing, when Juan
noticed her missing and panicked.
We were used to that, we'd each
known him to ring us at all hours,
asking for her. She was a bee
that garnered her honey elsewhere,
not just at home. She slipped away
while the Scottish diva was singing
a German lament. She wore red,
I remember, a knee-length dress
that brought out her black hair.
She'd over-rouged her cheeks.
When the call came I took it –
I didn't look at Juan, just walked
to the car and drove to town,
like lava was following me.
I braked in the square, by the baker's,
and joined the crowd round the tree.
I saw the cut rope hanging there.
I waited, then pushed on through.

SKATING

You'll never be seen skating
on a frozen lake, arms folded,
wearing your hat and long coat,
a tight smile on your lips
as you look into the distance.
You won't even be standing,
looking on, pointing the camera,
the dog gurning beside you
behind his smoky breath,
and the laughter of children
who repeatedly fall, then get up
to skate on again, till night
hides the sky that's crammed
with the next snow. No, you
won't notice the night, stuck
as you'll be, in your blue room,
reading, listening to Coltrane
or Parker, getting up to grab
an oatcake or refill your glass
while outside the snow rises
imperceptibly, till it reaches
the roofs of the smaller houses,
and men and women in dressing-gowns
are skiing between chimneys,
creating a fluid geometry
under the blank-faced moon.

THE BAT

In through the open French window
flew the bat, past my head
as I stood peeing into the river
that flowed beneath the house
which the bat quickly explored, round
the barn-sized living-room,
up the cracked stairs, two flights
to the attic where the kids slept
but they wouldn't tonight, not while
the bat stayed. So we opened
the skylight, despite the wasp's nest
on the drainpipe, and I stood
with a glass of the local red wine,
calling to the bat, like Dracula,
Lovely creature of the night,
come to me, I am your friend,
while it looped the length of the room,
with the kids on the stairs, laughing,
but not coming in. And it stayed
past midnight, till Joan
cupped it in her hands
and carried it downstairs
to the same French window,
where I stood, calling after it,
Lovely creature of the night,
come back, I miss you,
come to me, I am your friend.

A PICNIC ON ICE

Let's go back to Mullett Lake in March
and have a picnic on the ice.
Let's wrap up like Inuits, and meet
three miles north of Indian River,
where the jetty stands in summer
front of 577 Grandview Beach.
We'll cram in Lynch's vintage hearse
and motor slowly out onto the ice,
where I'll spread my blue tablecloth
and as it darkens I'll line up bottles –
wine, Zubrovka, poteen if I can get it –
and onion bhajees, chilli beans, tortilla,
goats' cheese and five kinds of bread.
I'll bring a tape of Irish music
to charm the ghosts beneath the ice.
Some of you may act like Michiganders
and cut holes to fish through,
or slip through and swim underwater
like the mad Finns of Minnesota –
or maybe just make needle-holes of piss.
And we might just find time for stories,
the one about the team of horses
that fell through the ice in March –
the current changed, a seam opened,
the ice quaked, a foot became an inch –
and they're down there, skeletons in harness
to a sleigh of logs, past the sunken island's
northern shore, seen a couple times
by the seaplane pilot who told me
over steaks in the Hack-ma-Tack –
and if the ice should suddenly crack
we'll be tipsy, replete, comforted
to be sinking all together with a hearse
down to join the horse-bones on the bottom.

GHOST STORY

I will break into a tomb
in Highgate cemetery,
one that hasn't been opened
for a hundred years.
The bones in there won't mind.
I'll light a candle
and set up my camp bed,
then I'll read ghost stories
till the bones rattle
and come together
to form a skeleton.
I'll watch flesh form
on that skull again,
then the chest, the legs,
until a smiling old man
dressed in tweeds
sits down beside me
and asks me to read on.

UP ON THE ROOF

Up on the roof of a church
was a small, blond boy
and a black-and-white kitten.

Down below, the priest
was praying aloud,
pleading with God,

asking him to keep
this small boy from falling,
down from his church.

He couldn't phone the mother
as he didn't know her,
and cats all looked the same.

When the verger appeared
with a telescopic ladder
the priest closed his eyes

and, gripping his rosary,
he prayed in the dark until
the verger began to climb.

The boy was on his feet now
calling the kitten
who refused to move.

'Sit down,' begged the priest,
in an almost whisper
so as not to alarm the boy

who paid no attention,
walking over the slates
as if on the pavement

or as if he had wings –
with the sun in his hair
he looked like an angel.

When the verger's bald head
rose above the drainpipe
the boy had the kitten

and was walking back,
along the ridge,
with a beatific smile.

THE TUNNEL

When they opened the manhole
on the street outside our house
I wanted to climb into it.
I could hear the rats calling.
I could hear the smugglers
manhandling kegs of ale.
I could hear the engine
of a midget U-boat
making inroads from the sea,
and behind it, whispered German,
what these bored submariners
were saying they'd do.
I knew the tunnel went on
down the length of Ireland
and I could row for weeks
in my homemade dingy
before I'd hit the southern coast,
with my strapped-on torch
getting weaker, my water
and sardines running out,
but already I could see
the walls lightening, hear gulls
at the tunnel's end, then the strange
accents of Cork fishermen
who stood and watched me emerge.

THE TOMBS

Looking over the tombs at the cathedral,
listening to the ringing of the bells,
I see again *The Resurrection, Cookham*
only this time it's moving, not still.
I watch my granny climb out of one tomb,
younger than I ever saw her, and slimmer,
brushing the dust from her breasts,
looking round for someone to talk to.
And there, suddenly, is pregnant Doris
with the red marks gone from her neck.
And that has to be my father-in-law
standing with my grandfather, eyeing
the cathedral wall, both smoking
untipped cigarettes, till Raymond Tyner
calls them, in his drawl, to follow him
under the yew trees, out of sight,
and I rush down the stairs to meet them
but there's no one between me and the tombs.

THE LAKE

The man stood at the edge of the lake
at dawn. Behind him, in a field,
a scarecrow's rags fluttered in the wind
while a sleepy owl gave a last call.
The man stood there, as if made out of stone.
Only he could have told he was blind.

It was a lake like this had made him blind,
a similar-sized, though much warmer lake
in a province ruled over by a stone
god who'd stood in a sacred field,
and who'd banished, forever, the wind
that ancestors had said used to call –

and when a big wind comes to call
it takes the houses away. Being blind
he could easily see this, and the wind
was red, not like this northern lake-
wind that came over the grassy fields
with all the colour of grey stone.

The man bent down and picked up a stone
which he threw in the lake. A call
echoed out over the water and fields,
long and plangent. It isn't easy being blind
and standing at the edge of a lake
in a cold and unseasonable wind,

standing there, wishing you could wind
back to days when you *saw* the stones
you threw in a very different lake,
to the screeches of monkeys, the calls
of parrots – the reckless, blind
assumption that days in the fields

would always be like this, and fields
would stay bare and brown, no wind
buffeting scarecrows, a god of stone
that didn't save you from going blind
because of a worm that swam in the lake,
and a mother that rushed to your wild calls.

The man stood there. Behind him, fields,
winds away, he heard those wild calls
when his eyes turned blind, turned to stone.

THE ATTIC

I've finished my mural of you naked,
and only I will see it.
The sun streams through the skylight,
lighting your face, your breasts.
I lie in the hammock remembering
the afternoon hours I spent with you
up here, where no one goes.
We'd have Van Morrison singing
low down, and sometimes wine.
Always there'd be a vase of flowers
in the corner, on the trunk –
you'd smuggle them up the stairs
until you closed that black door
and the rest of the house wasn't there.
I remember the day we fell asleep
until they came looking for us –
my mother calling my name,
but not coming up. We waited
till all was quiet, then reappeared
in the living room, and sat apart,
like we had to, for half an hour –
the longest you spent down there –
then I went with you to the door.
I wouldn't accompany you to the bus stop,
instead went back upstairs
to lie there in the growing dark,
listening to Van over and over again.
I must have known you'd never return.
It was weeks before I started the mural,
and I took my time, I wanted *you* there,
on my wall, right in every detail,
looking as if I could lift you down.
I wanted you, and now I've got you

and you'll never go downstairs.
Tomorrow I'll paint a vase of flowers,
irises, to match your eyes,
but tonight I'm sleeping here,
the first night I'll have spent with you.

WADING

She's in the sea again.
She's got her white dress on.
She's wading through the waves
watched by no one.
The stars are blotted out
and the moon's hidden,
and she's splashing through the sea
thinking about him.

He was here an hour ago.
He ran along the beach.
He shouted out 'Julie!'
and waved a torch
but he never came her way
and she ignored him,
stood there and watched
as he staggered home.

Her eyes are pebbles.
Her dress is seaweed.
Her legs are driftwood
that needs to float,
but for now she keeps wading,
slicing the waves
that keep on offering
their myriad loves.

THE FLIES

i.m. Miroslav Holub

The flies were dying that day.
I found the first one in my hair
as I sat in the train from Cambridge,
and when I lugged my bags
through King's Cross Station
I had to stop and brush away
a fly who'd picked my face
as the last place to land on.
A third fell on my head
at the taxi-stand, and then I knew
they were dying for you, Miroslav,
or you were each of them,
pestering me, to prove you'd died,
eaten by that swift,
fleeing from the fires of Estrées.

THE APPOINTMENT

After he'd crossed seven borders
on trains, in cars, on foot,
and each language he heard
meant less to him than the last,
he came to a wooded lake,
and he knew, looking at it,
that in winter it froze over,
that people walked across it
to the island in the middle
where bonfires were lit
and dozens danced and sang
to fresh-made music,
laughing amid the snow –
he knew, because he'd seen this
in a recurring dream,
and he'd been among them
dancing alone.

And now he'd come here
but not in winter,
so he jumped in and swam,
and a red-tailed hawk
led him to the island,
where among the silver birch
he found a lantern
and a two-stringed guitar
which he practised on
till he plucked out a jig
that set his feet tapping
and got him singing,
louder and louder,

out across the water
to the listening town –
when he lit the lantern
he knew the boats would come.

THE VOLCANO

When they phoned to tell us
the volcano was finally erupting,
we threw a few things in a bag –
your best sari, my Armani suit –
grabbed the monkey and ran.
For a minute the car wouldn't start,
then we were off, rattling
down that mountain road, the stench
of sulphur in the air, you
whitefaced and silent at the wheel.
When you took a corner too quickly
and the car nearly turned over
the monkey started screeching,
so I crooned that country song
it loved, turning to look behind me
to see if lava was following
but all I saw was
a herd of donkeys, galloping,
and the sky filled with crows,
as if the mountain was emptying
of all its creatures, and all,
including us, would get away.
And as you slowed down
I put my hand on yours and squeezed,
thinking of the lava
entering our house
and swarming over the chairs,
turning them into sculptures
that one day we'd come back and see.

BLUE TRAIN

Standing in the soggy queue,
waiting for the piper to arrive
and lead us to the station
where we'll board a train for Vienna,
a special blue train,
with a small original Picasso
in every compartment, and no
stops for strangers to join,
no police to scrutinise passports,
only the finest Czech beer
free in the restaurant car,
and *Wiener Schnitzel, Apfelstrudel,*
and smiling young women
fluent in three languages
to bring you what you need.

But the piper is late, and the rain
is increasing, and I've only
Czech money, and I can't shake off
the image that hijacked last night –
a couple doing it, on a bench
in full view of anyone
who chose that park to walk through
as I did – it wasn't late,
and they didn't care – so now
I need that blue train
to spirit me south, away from
Prague and its appetites,
the young in one another's laps,
clothes in disarray, but no train
will wait on the platform all day.

FRANCE

In the middle of cooking an Indian meal,
he remembers a summer night in France –
the stars were falling through the sky,
and the day's premonition had been hailstones,
big as mothballs, denting the car.
Whether that was a cause or not, they'd had
a row to remember, or forget, after
the meal – *magrets de canard*, marinated,
sizzled on the barbecue, served pink –
then the recriminations started,
flying around as mad as the stars above,
and as this continued the toilet gave way,
raining unclean water through the ceiling,
while shouts echoed, till she retired,
leaving him to sit there in the garden,
in the clammy night, on the cognac now,
replaying every harsh word she'd said
while the stars got sense and settled overhead.

GUARDIAN OF THE WOMEN'S LOO IN WATERLOO

Centimes, francs – I've a drawer full of them.
I'm not supposed to take them but I do.
At least they pay, these French women.
They don't stand there, smirking, saying
I'm broke, I'm going to wet myself,
or worse, vaulting over the metal bar
to run and lock themselves in a cubicle.
As if I'd leave my seat to stop them!

The things that go on behind me, sometimes –
sex, drugs-dealing, even a murder, once.
It's not my job to police the joint.
That's Angela's territory, when she's here.
More often than not she's doing the rounds,
but I like it when I get to talk to her,
hear her gossip, who's bonking who
in the disused waiting room on platform 12.

Sometimes she calls me back to show me
what's been left behind – knickers,
puke, a used condom (I let no men in!)
a lipstick-smeared photo of Brad Pitt.
Once there was the name Steve in blood
all over the back of the door, but the saddest,
the one that stayed with me, was a dead baby
propped up in the corner, wearing a bow.

I tell you, I want out from time to time.
The Eurostar's just across the platform,
I could go to Paris and not come back,
lose myself in Montmartre, an artist's flat
overlooking steps, but who'd take over, who'd be

guardian of the women's loo in Waterloo,
with all the tact, let live, let go by, that's needed?
20p entrance? That's half of it. The skill's in the rest.

LONG DISTANCE

At the fifth ring, just as the ansaphone clicks in,
I drop the groceries, the clanking bottles, and grab the phone.
'Ah, Herr Sweeney, endlich sind Sie da!'
German! I haven't heard those sounds in some time.
I send a message to my voicebox to dredge up
a few sentences from the sub-spittle debris of what's gone
but while I'm waiting, that German voice speaks again:
'Hören Sie mich nicht, Herr Sweeney? Was ist los, Mann?'
'Entschuldigung,' I splutter, 'Mein Deutsch ist verschwunden.'
'Quatsch!' barks the firm male voice, 'Sie sind nur faul.'
And I nod, as the creaky translation filters through.
Once, for three brief months, I thought in German –
had to translate from the English I'd grown up in.
'Ja, wirklich,' I say, 'Ich bin eine Schande!'
'Stimmt,' says the cross man, 'Gut dass Sie verstehen.'
And before I can find a few simple words to reply,
'Bis nächstes Mal, dann – und ich werde Sie wieder anrufen,'
then, abruptly, he is gone, no 'Tschüss',
or 'Auf Wiederhören'. I immediately press 1471 –
I want his number, want to know where he's rung from,
but *the caller has withheld his number* is what I get,
so, shaking, I replace the receiver and go straight out again.

OUR RESIDENT

Hiding the gun
in the half-full laundry basket,
he takes the stairs two at a time
to the front door.
Another long double ring,
then he has it open.
No, it isn't a constable
nor is it his wife home,
saying she forgot her keys.
It's a perfume salesman
in a lime-green jacket,
whom of course he invites in.
Seated on the sofa,
the glass table pulled up,
the man spreads his wares
while our resident makes coffee,
whispering to himself
in the blue-tiled kitchen.
He peers in at the stranger,
closing one eye, and thinks
what a mess the blood would make
of the sofa, and how would he
dispose of the body.
The first pleasant pong
distracts him, then they're all
sprayed, one by one,
on his hands and ingested
till the coffee tastes
of perfume, and he gets
his chequebook and buys
five at the special price,
then accompanies the man
to the door of the flat

where the laundry basket sits,
and it would be simple
to shoot him in the back
going down the stairs,
but the gun stays buried,
our resident has decided
its first shot will not be yet.

THE HOUSEBOAT

'Did Dick Blackstaff do it?
Is he the fucker we want?'
We banged on the hatch of that houseboat,
under a blood-red moon,
while a police siren weaved among the flats
and a dog howled till a shot rang out.
But we heard no sound from the cabin,
no whisper, or muffled step,
so we banged again, and shouted
'Blackstaff, if you're in there
come out and clear your name.'
And these words rang over the water
to the wreck of the tanker
where the kids hung out in the summer
but now was as bare as a crag.
And the houseboat rocked, as the wind
whipped up the incoming tide,
and brought with it the smell of curry
from 'The Star of Malibar'.
'Tell Blackstaff there's a bullet
waiting for his skull,' we shouted
before jumping back to land
and cramming in Jack's Audi
for the short ride home.

THE ZOOKEEPER'S TROUBLES

for Tom Lynch

Riesfeldt, the zookeeper, was troubled,
so after work, when the rain cleared,
he took himself out to the orchard
and walked there among the apple trees,
in the dreamy silence that precedes dusk,
thinking of the problem that haunted him.
Why hadn't he stayed a rose-gardener?
Roses didn't need regular habits,
but his buck-elephant, Stefan, did
and, despite the soul-food of berries
figs and prunes, by the bushel,
and twenty-two doses of laxative,
Stefan's private complication persisted.
For Riesfeldt's wife it was a sport,
for him it was an incitement to violence,
but he rode this, he was a survivor,
and brought to work the next morning
an abundance of extra-virgin olive oil
which he administered in an enema.
He was not prepared for his success –
the sheer force of Stefan's defecation
knocked him to the ground, his head
hitting a rock, and he lay there
while two hundred pounds of dung
formed a mountain on top of him.
It took hours to clean up the remains.

ANIMALS

> *A narrative is all right so long as the narrator sticks*
> *to words as simple as dog, horse, sunset.*
> —Ezra Pound

Admit it, you wanted to shoot that dog
who stood barking on the edge of town,
right from the start of sunset, until
the clock in the square struck twelve
and the hotel's horse started to whinny,

sending you out from your musty bed
to the window that you flung open,
before sticking your head out and shouting
in bad French, 'Fuck off, animals,
some of us are trying to sleep here!'

At that, the dog barked louder, faster,
and the horse galloped round the field,
and a rooster, fooled by the noise,
began crowing, and two cats fought
openly, on an adjacent wall.

Closing the window was all you could do,
that and turning on the shower until
the animals were lost in the hiss,
and you slept there on the bathroom floor
till light brought the squawking of gulls.

ROADKILL

Scrape the cat off the road,
take it home and fillet out the flesh,
throw it in the marinade
where the deer you wrecked your bumper on
a week before Xmas, sits
in chunks, alongside slivers of fox,
a boned, de-spined hedgehog,
the legs and breasts of a slow hare –
all in a bath of red wine
with onion slices and garlic,
and an ounce of juniper berries.
That cat was the last ingredient
you didn't know you needed
and had better keep secret.
After a day, strain the marinade
and cook the meat all morning
in the wine and blood.
Serve in bowls, with bread.

A SMELL OF FISH

A smell of fish filled the valley
and all the seagulls came inland.

Cats ran everywhere, sniffing.
Men checked the level of the sea.

Some could be heard hammering.
Churches filled to pray for wind.

THE MOTHS

Or poem beginning with a line by Diane Di Prima

In the snow the moths walk stiffly,
they don't even try to fly.
Their footprints fill in as they make them,
as they follow one another home
up the cold poles of streetlamps
to wait there for the light.
Each dusk there's less of them,
and all more tired than before
but still they raise their voices
to greet the glowing filament –
first orange, then yellow
like their eyes. And the snow
gathers on their folded wings,
making them heavy, making some
fall to be crunched under boots,
or eaten by a passing dog,
while behind them, more walk stiffly
following the dead ones home.

ABANDONED

After two days he knew they were lying,
they wouldn't send anyone to rescue him,
he was stuck here, forever, on the moon
without even a dead man for company.
Why did they load so much dust and rocks
the module couldn't lift off?
How many experiments could they do?
How long before he'd replace some of the dust?
He looked up at Earth where his wife was.
What would they say to her? More lies,
he knew. His children would never learn
he hadn't died in a meteor shower,
and neither of them would visit his grave.
He wouldn't even have a grave!
He countered this by thinking back
to the last time he and his wife
had made love, to the borsch she'd cooked
that night, the vodka they'd drunk.
What was she doing now? Did she
know he was beaming thoughts at her
across the thousands of miles of space,
hoping that in her sleep she'd beam some back?

SIPPING FRASCATI IN CASTEL GANDOLFO

for Padraig Rooney

Arriving by seaplane on the lake
down the hill from Castel Gandolfo,
you'll have time to sit in the square
with a glass or two of chilled Frascati
and sneak glances at the Pope's palace,
the two Swiss guards in the doorway
with their pikes and clownish uniforms,
and if you sit there long enough
the man himself might come out
in a sharp black suit (Armani,
not Michelangelo), dark glasses on,
the bodyguards well behind him,
and you'll nod to him as he pauses
long enough for a snifter of vodka,
then shuffles off to his regular table
at the lakeside restaurant he prefers
to any other, where they cook
what he requests the previous night,
and where no one approaches him
except the *padrone*'s daughter
who reads him the poems of Goethe,
three an evening, then he signs
to the minders it's time to leave,
and soon he's back at the palace,
and if you're still sitting there
you can toast him as he goes in.

DO NOT THROW STONES AT THIS SIGN

Do not throw stones at this sign
which stands here, in a stony field
a stone's throw from the sea
whose beach is a mess of pebbles
since the sand was stolen for building,
and the few people who dawdle there,
rods in hand, catch nothing,
not even a shoe – might as well
bombard the waves with golfballs,
or wade in and hold their breath,
or bend, as they do, and grab a handful
of pebbles to throw at the sign,
and each time they hit it they cheer
and chalk up another beer, especially
the man who thought up the sign,
who got his paintbrush and wrote
'Do Not Throw Stones At This Sign'
on a piece of driftwood which he stuck
in this useless field, then, laughing,
danced his way to the house of beer.

IN THE ICE

When we were down in the dark hole
far beneath the giant's feet,
and I was still looking up the wall
I heard a voice say, 'Watch out,
mind you don't tramp on the heads
of your miserable, weary brothers.'
I turned and saw I was walking on
a frozen lake – the ice far thicker
than the Danube ever gets, or Don,
so thick Everest could fall on it
without making a crack. And as a frog
sits with its head out of water
to croak, so these ghosts were stuck
up to their necks in the ice,
each making a noise like a stork
and keeping his face hidden. I saw
at my feet two melded together,
so much they had the one hair.
'Tell me,' I said, 'who you are.'
They raised their faces, and cried
tears that froze at once, locking
their eyes, then they butted each other.
And one who'd lost both his ears
to the cold, asked, 'Why do you stare at us?'
'Those, if you want to know, were twins,
treacherous brothers who killed each other,
but we're all treacherous here.'
Then I saw a thousand faces
turned to dogs' faces by the cold,
as, shivering, I walked through the heads
and straight into one. The shouts of it!
'What are you doing tramping on me?

What have I ever done to you?'
'Who do you think you are?' I said,
'to speak like that. Look at yourself.'
'No, who are you?' he answered,
'walking here, kicking me in the face.'
'I'm alive,' I said, 'and if you want fame
I can get you it. What's your name?'
'Fame is the last thing I want.
Fuck off and don't annoy me further.
Flattery doesn't work down here.'
I took him by the hair and said,
'Give me your name or I'll bald you.'
'Do if you want but I still won't say
who I am.' I tore out a handful,
then another, and he barked like a dog.
'What's wrong, Bocca?' another shouted.
Are your grinding teeth not enough for you?
What devil's making you bark?'
'Ha, you can keep quiet now,' I said,
'for despite you I know who you are.'
'Fuck off,' he answered, 'tell what you will
but tell about that fucker who spoke, too –
say you saw Buoso in the place
where the sinners are sent to freeze,
and if you're asked who else was there
you can name a certain Papal Legate
whose throat Florence slit,
also one Gianni de Soldanier,
and Ganelon, and Tribaldetto –
traitors every fucking one.'
We'd gone on ahead when I saw
two frozen in the one hole, one's teeth
clamped on the other's head.
'What kind of show of hatred is this?'
I asked. 'What has this fellow done

to make you want to eat him? Tell me
and I'll avenge you in the upper world,
if my tongue will still be able to speak.'

(*Inferno*, XXXII, 16-139)

INCIDENT IN EXETER STATION

for Eddie Linden

He came in the door, staring at me,
like he'd known me in another life.
'I've chased everywhere after you,' he said.
'Years and years, I've been on the road,
too many to count. The train-fares,
the bus-fares, the plane-fares ...
The least you can do is buy me a pint.'
He plonked his duffle-bag on the floor
and sat on the stool next to mine.
He looked in my eyes like a holy man,
said, 'You're looking well, you've lost weight.'
His face could have done with flesh.
His hair needed a cut and a wash.
'I don't know you,' I said, 'I've never,
ever seen you before.' He smiled,
the same smile Jesus must have flashed
at Judas, then his face changed
into a voodoo mask, as he shouted,
'After all I've done for you!',
turning to face the roomful of eaters
and drinkers, all of whom ignored him
but I knew they classed us together,
so, seeing a train pull up at the platform,
I grabbed my hat, bags and ran,
getting in just as the train was leaving,
not knowing where it was headed,
hearing his roars follow me out
into the green Devon countryside
that I'd never risk visiting again.

WITNESS

Or poem beginning with a line by Shelley

A man who was about to hang himself
saw strange lights in the sky.
He carried on making the perfect noose
but the lights kept dancing, like fireflies.
Why didn't they go elsewhere, he thought.
They were darting so fast here and there
and making triangular motions,
and they kept changing colour, too –
first white, then blue, then red.
The man threw his rope on the ground
as the lights zoomed close, then off again
before stopping and forming a triangle
which hung there above his head,
dropping slowly, till he could make out
the black shape the lights hung beneath –
clearly, some amazing craft of the sky
sent here for him to witness,
and he crossed himself, standing there
as the lights took off again, faster
than a shout, and soon were gone
beyond the edge of the firmament,
leaving stars that were fixed
and clouds scudding across the moon,
nothing to substantiate what he'd seen
but he'd seen it, and whistled his horse
to take him the dark road home.

SEA DANCE

i.m. Ted Hughes

The sea is wild tonight,
and the darkness sitting down on it
doesn't calm it. The ships
are skulking in the ports.
Only the barnacled bones of the drowned
are flailing through waves,
doing that dance no one sees,
that rolling and twisting underwater,
and tonight's guest-spot
goes to the newest drowner –
a jumper off Dunwich cliff
on a night milder than this,
his torch left lit on the top,
his dog howling.
                              And eels
have had his eyes, and enjoyed them,
cod have nibbled his stiff flesh,
bass have bared his foot-bones
but all this only helps him –
he has never moved so freely
or heard such fierce music,
or covered so many miles
in so few hours, and who knows
where this sea will bring him,
what coast it will dump him on,
or maybe a net will catch him
but first the sea must finish
its war, let the rising sun
bounce beams off its glassy surface,
let the bones settle on the bottom
until the next storm
when the dance will begin.

SWIMMER

For the umpteenth time I looked out at the sea
but there was nothing to catch my eye,
just a man wheeling a barrow up the beach.
I looked again, frisking the whole expanse
for a ship, a boat, any floating debris
but all I saw was a cat in the marram grass
slinking towards three rabbits playing.
The waves were apologetic on the shingle,
after the excesses of the previous night,
and the sun had lit a strip of the horizon.
All the scene needed was one small boat

but stubbornly none came. Then suddenly,
a mile or so out, I saw a swimmer –
there was no mistaking that bobbing head.
I rummaged in every drawer in the house
but none held binoculars. I ran upstairs again.
He or she was still there – it was a *she*,
I decided, and she'd made this swim before.
This was a training run for the big one –
across the Atlantic. That was why
no boats were in attendance, no copters
overhead, no paparazzi on the beach, waiting.

Up above me the roofers were hammering
as if nothing was happening. I heard a laugh
and thought of the woman in the water.
She'd be tired, hungry, cold. It was up to me
to meet her with a towel, bring her back
to my radiators and a scorching coffee,
maybe a bath, if she could still stand water.
I went to the window to see if she was near
but she'd gone, there was no head there!
I ran out, and down the lane to the beach.
The sea sent small waves to break at my feet.

SWEENEY

Even when I said my head was shrinking
he didn't believe me. Change doctors, I thought,
but why bother? We're all hypochondriacs,
and those feathers pushing through my pores
were psychosomatic. My wife was the same
till I pecked her, trying to kiss her, one morning,
scratching her feet with my claws, cawing
good morning till she left the bed with a scream.

I moved out then, onto a branch of the oak
behind the house. That way I could see her
as she opened the car, on her way to work.
Being a crow didn't stop me fancying her,
especially when she wore that short black number
I'd bought her in Berlin. I don't know if she
noticed me. I never saw her look up.
I did see boxes of my books going out.

The nest was a problem. My wife had cursed me
for being useless at DIY, and it was no better now.
I wasn't a natural flier, either, so I sat
in that tree, soaking, shivering, all day.
Every time I saw someone carrying a bottle of wine
I cawed. A takeaway curry was worse.
And the day I saw my wife come home
with a man, I flew finally into our wall.

URINE THERAPY

After the needles, the yoga, he turned to urine therapy
so each morning he rose and peed into a pint glass
then downed it in one. At first it was difficult not to gag
but he kept in his head the image of the 120 year old
Japanese man who ascribed his longevity to drinking his pee
every morning since the day of his 21st birthday,
and who came across, on TV, as being fitter than a flea.

And he collected the writings of John W. Armstrong
who'd developed the therapy in the 1930s
as a way of cleansing the body by reingesting toxins –
an ingenious and impertinent double bluff, he thought
and imagined John W's first tentative sipping
of the warm, newly delivered, deep yellow liquid
behind the securely locked door of his bathroom.

No, he would never let a taste and a smell beat him,
and soon the variants in both led him to nudge
his diet to the bolder peripheries – curries, garlic,
asparagus, of course, the lemon grass and rotted shrimp
of Thailand, sashimi, chili and basil, cabbage –
and along with the assortment of freshly squeezed juices
he slipped in the odd whisky or brandy nightcap

to give the slightest of frissons to that first sip
the following morning, and bring a smile to the face
behind which all the illnesses he was ruling out
were being listed, and all the extra years he'd live
were being added up, and all the wrongfooted toxins
were unwittingly working so hard for him
before his grapefruit, his coffee, his wholemeal toast and jam.

THE ANNIVERSARY CHOIR

for my parents

Sing loud, cry out, be of good cheer
for the anniversary is here.
'Which one?' asked a crippled cat.
'The fiftieth, how's that?'

'Fifty? That's nothing' said the yew tree
stood on the edge of the cemetery.
But the stiff cat shook her head
and a passing snail agreed.

Then a crow came flapping through the sky
and his harsh voice did say
'Fifty years is quite a while!'
And his beak cracked into a smile.

And out of the ground came a dead dog
who sprouted flesh again and spoke:
'That's as long as I was alive
if you multiplied it by five.'

And the sea itself rumbled a roar
and flung an old boot on the shore –
'It's a gift', a gull explained,
'It belonged to a friend

who's sadly unable to be here
but if you sit the boot on a chair
his ghost will raise a glass to you
just like the rest of us do.'

And all the other ghosts said aye
and waved invisibly from the sky.
And the moon, who's been walked on,
winked at the hidden sun.

FROG-TAMING

Any fool can learn to catch a frog –
the trick is to do it blindfolded,
lying there, in the wet grass,
listening for the hop and the croak.

And the real trick is to keep it alive,
not strangle it, or squeeze it dead –
that way you can take it home
and tame it, make it your pet.

But early on, keep the cat locked up.
Soon she'll get used to her odd sibling –
meanwhile put a bit of time into
picking a suitable name for a frog.

And research a frog's ideal diet,
also the best sleeping arrangement –
water somewhere nearby, of course,
and plenty of air, plenty of air.

Be sure to play the frog the right music
so it can learn hopping tricks –
ones it can reproduce on the cleared table
when you have dinner guests around,

while you find your blindfold and put it on,
holding your hands out and grasping
the air the frog has just vacated –
making it clear you're deliberately missing.

SANCTUARY

Stay awhile. Don't go just yet.
The sirens are roaming the streets,
the stabbing youths are out in packs,
there's mayhem in the tea-leaves.
You're much better off staying here.
I have a Bordeaux you'll like,
let's open it. (I've a second bottle, too.)
And goat's cheese to fast for,
also a blue from the Vale of Cashel –
and the source of the bread stays secret.
Was I expecting you to stay?
No, I always eat like this.
Hear that – wasn't it a gunshot?
Come closer, turn the music up.
Maybe we should dim the lights.
Let's clink our glasses to each other
if no better toast comes to mind.
I told you you'd ooh! at the cheese –
here, have some more. A top up?
You're the kind of girl I like.
Listen, that was definitely a bomb.
Maybe the civil war has started,
the one they've all been promising.
Well, there's nowhere to go now,
so let's kill the lights and retire.